Gooseberry Patch®

Christmas
COOKIE
JAR

A Country Store In Your Mailbox®

Gooseberry Patch
600 London Road
P.O. Box 190
Delaware, OH 43015

www.gooseberrypatch.com

1·800·854·6673

Do you have a tried & true recipe...
tip, craft or memory that you'd like to see featured in a **Gooseberry
Patch** cookbook? Visit our website at **www.gooseberrypatch.com**,
register and follow the easy steps to submit your favorite family recipe.
Or send them to us at:

Gooseberry Patch
Attn: Cookbook Dept.
P.O. Box 190
Delaware, OH 43015

Don't forget to include the number of servings your recipe makes,
plus your name, address, phone number and e-mail address.
If we select your recipe, your name will appear right along with
it...and you'll receive a **FREE** copy of the book!

CONTENTS

Dedication

To everyone who still leaves
milk & cookies for Santa...
Merry Christmas!

Appreciation

For all of you who reached into
family recipe boxes to share tried
& true favorites...thanks!

Simply Divine
DROP COOKIES

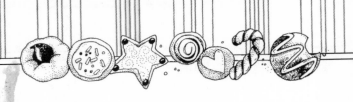

Ready, Set, Bake!

Start a list of must-have cookies to bake...remember to ask family members for their favorites too!

° ❄ °

Make a list of ingredients you'll need, check supplies on hand and start to stock up. Sugar, flour, spices, butter and nuts usually go on sale by Thanksgiving...butter and nuts can even be frozen for the freshest flavor.

° ❄ °

If the baking powder and baking soda in the cupboard are from last Christmas, it's best to replace them...spices too.

° ❄ °

Take it easy! Spread baking and decorating over a few days or even weekends. Make all the dough one day and refrigerate it to bake the next day...even freeze dough and then do your baking on following weekends, as time allows.

° ❄ °

On baking days, pop an easy dinner in the slow cooker first thing in the morning. Then relax and enjoy baking... dinner will be ready whenever you are.

Simply Divine **DROP COOKIES**

Frosted Ginger Creams

Judy Adams
Wooster, OH

A co-worker shared this yummy recipe with me.

1/2 c. margarine, softened
1 c. sugar
1 egg, beaten
1 c. light molasses
4 c. all-purpose flour
2 t. baking soda
1/2 t. salt

2 t. cinnamon
2 t. ground ginger
1 t. ground cloves
1 t. nutmeg
1 c. hot water
Garnish: vanilla frosting

Mix together all ingredients except frosting in a large bowl. Drop by teaspoonfuls onto greased baking sheets. Bake at 400 degrees for 8 minutes. Frost with vanilla frosting. Makes 8 dozen.

Fill a dainty vintage teacup with bite-size cookies
for a sweet "pick-me-up" gift.

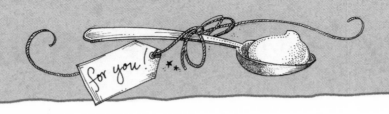

Peppery Molasses Cookies

Lisa Ashton
Aston, PA

These are really spicy...the black pepper gives them a kick!

3/4 c. butter, softened
3/4 c. sugar
1 egg
1/4 c. molasses
2 c. all-purpose flour

2 t. baking soda
1 t. cinnamon
1/2 t. salt
1-1/2 t. pepper
Garnish: additional sugar

Combine butter and sugar in a large bowl until fluffy. Beat in egg; add molasses. Whisk together flour and remaining ingredients. Gradually add to butter mixture; mix well. Form into one-inch balls and roll in sugar. Arrange 2 inches apart on ungreased baking sheets. Bake at 350 degrees for 12 to 15 minutes. Remove and cool on wire rack. Makes 4 to 5 dozen.

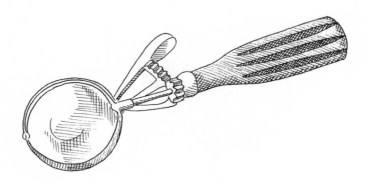

Use a mini ice cream scoop for perfectly portioned
drop cookies...you'll be done in a jiffy!

Pfeffernusse

Jane E. Granger
Manteno, IL

You'll want to eat these tiny cookies by the handful!

1 c. butter, softened
1 c. sugar
2 eggs, beaten
1 t. cinnamon
1/2 t. nutmeg
1/4 t. ground cloves
1/4 t. allspice
1/4 c. anise seed

1/2 c. corn syrup
1/2 c. molasses
1/3 c. water
1 t. baking soda
6-2/3 c. all-purpose flour
5 c. powdered sugar
1/2 c. warm water

Combine butter and sugar in a large bowl. Add eggs and spices; mix well. In a separate bowl, combine corn syrup, molasses, water and baking soda. Add to butter mixture. Stir in flour; mix well. Chill for at least one hour, until firm. Roll into 3/4-inch balls and arrange on greased baking sheets. Bake at 350 degrees for 10 to 15 minutes. Cool for a few minutes. Mix powdered sugar and warm water to make a glaze consistency. Drop cooled cookies into glaze, a few at a time; place on wire racks to dry. Makes 9 to 9-1/2 dozen.

Parchment paper is a baker's best friend. Place it on a baking sheet to keep cookies from spreading and sticking...clean-up is a breeze too! Look for rolls of parchment paper at groceries and bakery supply stores.

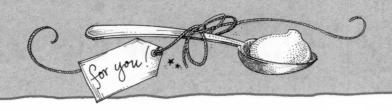

Gumdrop Jewels

Stacey Roth
Clark, MO

Grandma Betty always makes these cookies at Christmastime.
We all want to take some home...if there are any left!

1 c. shortening
1 c. brown sugar, packed
1 c. sugar
2 eggs, beaten
1 t. vanilla extract
1/4 t. salt
1 t. baking powder
1 t. baking soda
2 c. all-purpose flour
1 c. gumdrops, chopped
1 c. chopped nuts
2 c. quick-cooking oats,
   uncooked

Combine shortening, sugars and eggs; beat until smooth. Stir in remaining ingredients. Drop by rounded teaspoonfuls onto ungreased baking sheets. Bake at 350 degrees for 10 to 12 minutes. Makes 2-1/2 to 3 dozen.

Rolling dough into cookie-size balls is child's play...perfect for kids learning to bake. Make a sample dough ball so they'll know what size to make, set out baking sheets and let the kids take over!

Holiday Fruit Cookies

Sharon Crider
Junction City, KS

Toss the candied fruit with a little of the flour...
it'll be much easier to chop!

2-1/4 c. all-purpose flour
1 t. baking soda
1/2 t. salt
1 c. butter, softened
2-3/4 c. brown sugar, packed
3/4 c. sugar

2 eggs, beaten
1 t. vanilla extract
2 c. crispy rice cereal
1 c. mixed candied fruit, finely
   chopped

Mix together flour, baking soda and salt; set aside. Beat together butter and sugars in a large bowl; beat until well blended. Add eggs and vanilla; beat well. Gradually add flour mixture until well mixed. Stir in cereal and candied fruit. Drop by teaspoonfuls onto ungreased baking sheets. Bake at 350 degrees for about 10 minutes. Cool for 2 minutes before removing from baking sheets. Makes 6 dozen.

Give a cookie sampler! Place several yummy cookies in
each cup of a shiny new muffin tin.

Fancy Peppermint Puffs

Sherry Gordon
Arlington Heights, IL

My son always insists on smashing the candy canes for these cookies! Take a tip from me...place them in a plastic zipping bag first, so the bits won't fly all over the kitchen.

2 c. all-purpose flour
1/4 t. salt
1/2 c. butter, softened
1 c. powdered sugar
1 egg, beaten
1/2 t. peppermint extract

1/2 t. vanilla extract
8 1-oz. sqs. white baking
    chocolate, chopped
1 t. shortening
1/2 c. candy canes, crushed

Mix together flour and salt; set aside. Blend together butter and sugar in a large bowl until smooth and creamy. Stir in egg until well blended; add extracts. With an electric mixer on low speed, beat in flour mixture. Wrap in plastic wrap; chill for one hour. Form dough into one-inch balls and place on lightly greased baking sheets. Bake at 375 degrees for 10 to 12 minutes, until lightly golden. Cool completely on wire racks. Melt together chocolate and shortening; drizzle over cookies. Dip cookies in crushed candy; place on wax paper until set. Makes 3 dozen.

Turn flea-market finds into charming one-of-a-kind cookie stands. Use china and glass cement to attach a porcelain or glass plate atop a candleholder...so easy, you'll want to make some to share!

Mocha Meringues

*Carrie O'Shea
Marina Del Rey, CA*

*A new twist on old-fashioned "forgotten cookies"
that coffee lovers won't soon forget!*

1 t. vanilla extract
1 t. instant coffee granules
3 egg whites, at room
   temperature
1/4 t. cream of tartar

3/4 c. sugar
3 T. baking cocoa
1/2 c. mini semi-sweet chocolate
   chips

Stir together vanilla and coffee granules; set aside. With an electric mixer on medium speed, beat together egg whites and cream of tartar until frothy. Increase speed to medium-high; add sugar, one tablespoon at a time, and beat until stiff peaks form, about 5 minutes. Sprinkle cocoa over egg white mixture. Fold in cocoa with a wooden spoon until blended. Stir in vanilla mixture and chocolate chips. Drop by heaping tablespoonfuls onto parchment paper-lined baking sheets. Bake at 250 degrees for one hour without opening oven door. Turn oven off and tilt door open; leave cookies in oven for 30 minutes. Remove from oven; carefully lift cookies off with a thin metal spatula. Makes 3 dozen.

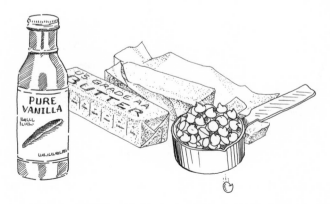

Look for clear vanilla extract in the baking aisle when
making white or light-colored cookies and candies.
It won't turn them dark like regular vanilla.

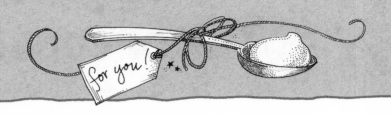

Shirley's Chocolate Chip Cookies

Jennie Gist
Gooseberry Patch

*Whenever we're leaving on a trip, I know we can count on
my mother-in-law to send along a tin filled with these
thin, crisp cookies. Thanks, Shirley!*

1/2 c. shortening
6 T. sugar
6 T. brown sugar, packed
1 egg, beaten
1/2 t. vanilla extract

1-1/8 c. all-purpose flour
1/2 t. baking soda
1/2 t. salt
1 c. semi-sweet chocolate chips

Blend together shortening and sugars; stir in egg and vanilla. Add
flour, baking soda and salt; mix well. Stir in chocolate chips. Drop by
teaspoonfuls onto ungreased baking sheets. Bake at 375 degrees for
10 to 12 minutes, until lightly golden. Makes about 4 dozen.

Start a notebook of your favorite tried & true cookie recipes! Each
Christmas, add notes about what worked well and what you'd do
differently. Remember to label family members' favorites...even add
snapshots of little bakers helping out. What a sweet tradition!

Oatmeal Crispies

Betty Moore
Mount Pleasant, IA

*My favorite cookies, ever since I first made them in my
junior high school Home Ec class! I've taken home many
blue ribbons from the county fair with these cookies.*

1 c. shortening
2 eggs, beaten
1 t. vanilla extract
1 c. brown sugar, packed
1 c. sugar
1-1/2 c. all-purpose flour
1 t. baking soda

1 t. salt
2 c. long-cooking oats,
  uncooked
Optional: 12-oz. pkg.
  semi-sweet chocolate
  or butterscotch chips,
  3/4 c. chopped nuts

Blend together shortening, eggs, vanilla and sugars; mix well.
In a separate bowl, combine flour, baking soda and salt; add to
shortening mixture. Stir in oats and optional ingredients, if using.
Drop by teaspoonfuls onto greased baking sheets. Bake at
350 degrees for 8 to 10 minutes. Makes 5 dozen.

Add toasty flavor to a favorite oatmeal cookie recipe. Spread
uncooked oats on a baking sheet and bake at 300 degrees for
8 to 10 minutes, until lightly golden. Let oats cool before
combining with other ingredients.

Grandpa's Famous Caramels

Susan Siemsen
Saginaw, MN

Every Christmas, our Ohio family looked forward to Grandpa Brown making these delicious caramels. He always made enough to give everyone a Christmas tin full...what a treat!

1 c. butter
2 c. light corn syrup
2 c. sugar
2 14-oz. cans sweetened
   condensed milk, divided

1/2 c. all-purpose flour
1 t. vanilla extract
1-1/2 c. chopped nuts

Melt butter in a heavy saucepan over medium heat. Add corn syrup and sugar; boil for 5 minutes, stirring constantly. Add 2-2/3 cups condensed milk. Mix flour with remaining condensed milk; add to saucepan. Boil, stirring constantly, until mixture darkens and reaches firm-ball stage, or 244 to 249 degrees on a candy thermometer. Remove from heat; stir in vanilla and nuts. Pour into a greased 13"x9" baking pan and cool completely. Cut into one-inch squares; wrap in wax paper. Makes 9-1/2 to 10 dozen pieces.

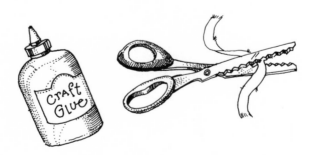

Family photos make terrific tags for cookie gifts. Just copy, cut out with decorative-edged scissors and tie on.

Espresso Bean Cookies

Kathy Grashoff
Fort Wayne, IN

Chocolate-covered coffee beans can be found at most neighborhood coffee shops in various package sizes. About 6 ounces equal one cup.

1/2 c. butter, softened
1/2 c. shortening
1/4 c. sugar
3/4 c. brown sugar, packed
2 eggs, beaten
1 t. vanilla extract
2-1/4 c. all-purpose flour
1 t. baking soda

1 t. salt
1/2 t. cinnamon
1 c. chopped almonds, toasted
1 c. chocolate-covered coffee beans
4 1.4-oz. toffee candy bars, chopped

With an electric mixer on medium speed, beat together butter and shortening until creamy. Gradually add sugars, beating well. Add eggs and vanilla; mix well. Combine flour, baking soda, salt and cinnamon. Add to butter mixture, beating well. Stir in almonds, coffee beans and chopped candy. Cover and chill dough until firm. Drop by heaping teaspoonfuls onto ungreased baking sheets. Bake at 350 degrees for 10 to 11 minutes, until golden. Cool on baking sheets for one minute. Remove to wire racks; cool completely. Makes 4 dozen.

Whenever you shop for cookie cutters, flavoring extracts, candy sprinkles and other baking supplies, toss a few extras in the shopping cart. Soon you'll have the makings of a gift basket for a friend who loves to bake...she'll really appreciate your thoughtfulness!

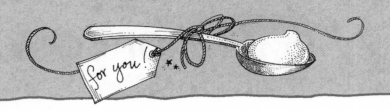

Southern Cream Cookies

Margie McCoin
Keizer, OR

I have fond memories of Mom making big double batches of these cookies. In a farm family with 7 kids, they didn't last long!

1 c. shortening
2 c. sugar
3 eggs, beaten
1 t. vanilla extract
1 c. sour cream

5 c. all-purpose flour
3/4 t. baking soda
1/2 to 1 t. salt
1 c. mini semi-sweet chocolate
  chips

Blend together shortening and sugar; beat in eggs and vanilla. Mix in sour cream and set aside. Whisk flour, baking soda and salt in a separate bowl. Add to shortening mixture; stir well. Add chocolate chips. Drop by teaspoonfuls onto ungreased baking sheets. Bake at 350 degrees for 15 minutes. Makes about 4 dozen.

Fresh-baked cookies should cool completely before storing,
to prevent softening and sticking together.

18

Buttery Ricotta Cookies

April Hale
Kirkwood, NY

This is a light, soft cookie...very yummy!

1/2 c. butter, softened
1/4 c. ricotta cheese
1 t. vanilla extract
1 c. sugar

1 egg, beaten
2 c. all-purpose flour
1/2 t. baking soda
1/2 t. salt

Blend together butter and ricotta cheese until creamy. Add vanilla; mix well. Gradually add sugar; stir in egg. Stir in remaining ingredients. Roll into one-inch balls and flatten slightly on greased baking sheet. Bake at 350 degrees for 10 minutes, or just until edges are golden. Remove to a wire rack to cool. Makes 20.

Lighten up a little...wrap gifts in the Sunday comics
or a page of crossword puzzles, just for fun!

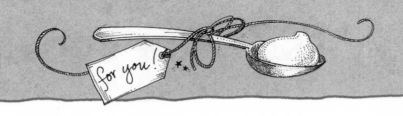

Mom's Gingersnaps

*Kim Jewett
Highland, UT*

*My mother shared this gingersnap recipe with me years ago
and now it wouldn't be Christmas without them.
They're delicious with a mug of hot chocolate.*

3/4 c. shortening
1 c. sugar
1/4 c. molasses
1 egg, beaten
2 c. all-purpose flour
2 t. baking soda

1/4 t. salt
1 t. ground ginger
1 t. ground cloves
1 t. cinnamon
Garnish: additional sugar

Blend together shortening and sugar. Add molasses and egg; beat
well. Add remaining ingredients except garnish; mix well. Form
teaspoonfuls of dough into balls; roll in sugar. Place 2 inches apart
on greased or parchment paper-lined baking sheets. Bake at
350 degrees for 12 to 15 minutes. Cool on a wire rack. Store in an
airtight container for chewy cookies or loosely covered for crisp
cookies. Makes 4 dozen.

For best results when baking cookies, set out butter
and eggs on the kitchen counter an hour ahead of
time, so they can come to room temperature.

4-Spice Crackles

Jo Ann

*The original recipe says these cookies will keep for
up to 2 weeks in an airtight container...but at
our house they never last that long!*

2-1/2 c. all-purpose flour
1 t. baking powder
1/2 t. baking soda
1/4 t. salt
1-1/2 t. ground ginger
1 t. ground cloves
1 t. nutmeg

1 t. cinnamon
1/2 c. butter, softened
1 c. brown sugar, packed
1/2 c. shortening
1/4 c. molasses
1 egg, beaten
2/3 c. sugar

Combine flour, baking powder, baking soda, salt and spices; set aside.
In a separate bowl, mix together butter, brown sugar and shortening;
stir in molasses and egg. Gradually add flour mixture until well
blended. Cover and chill at least 1-1/2 hours. Form into one-inch
balls; roll each ball in sugar. Place 2 inches apart on lightly greased
baking sheets; flatten slightly. Bake at 350 degrees for 9 to 12 minutes, until crackled and centers are soft. Cool on a wire rack. Makes
2 dozen.

Next time you pick up the Christmas cards in your mailbox, why not
tuck in a sweet treat for the letter carrier? You could even add a gift
card for a cup of coffee at a nearby coffee shop...it'll be much appreciated!

Raisin-Topped Drop Cookies

Linda Deal
Meyersdale, PA

This is a very old family recipe...I remember my mother, Gladys,
making these all the time when I was growing up. Yummy!

1 c. shortening
2 c. brown sugar, packed
2 eggs
1 t. vanilla extract

4 c. all-purpose flour
1 t. baking soda
5 T. milk

Blend together shortening and brown sugar; add eggs, one at a time.
Stir in vanilla. In a separate bowl, mix together flour and baking soda.
Add alternately with milk to shortening mixture; drop by tablespoonfuls onto greased baking sheets. With a spoon, spread batter to about
2 inches in diameter. Top with Raisin Topping. Bake at 375 degrees
for 10 minutes. Cool before removing from baking sheets. Makes
about 3 dozen.

Raisin Topping:

15-oz. pkg. raisins
1/2 c. sugar

2 T. all-purpose flour
1 t. lemon juice

Cover raisins with water in a saucepan. Simmer over medium heat for
10 minutes. Mix together sugar and flour; stir into raisins. Remove
from heat when thickened. Cool; stir in lemon juice.

Need a sleighful of gifts for
co-workers? Pick up vintage
coffee mugs at yard sales
for a song. Fill them with
cookies and wrap in festive
cellophane...sure to be a hit!

Old-Time Mincemeat Cookies

Annette Ingram
Grand Rapids, MI

Drizzle with a sweet lemon glaze...simply whisk together
3 cups powdered sugar and 1/4 cup lemon juice
until smooth.

1 c. shortening
1-1/2 c. brown sugar, packed
1 egg, beaten
2 c. mincemeat pie filling

3-1/4 c. all-purpose flour
1-1/2 t. baking soda
1/4 t. salt

Blend together shortening and brown sugar. Add egg and mincemeat; mix well. In a separate bowl, mix together flour, baking soda and salt; stir into mincemeat mixture. Drop by rounded teaspoonfuls onto ungreased baking sheets, 2 inches apart. Bake at 375 degrees for 8 to 10 minutes, until golden. Makes about 6 dozen.

Sweet table favors! Tuck a jumbo cookie inside a glassine envelope to set at each place setting...they'll love it!

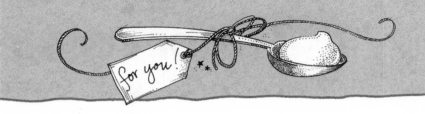

Lemon Delights

Tracey Varela
Thomasville, GA

*These cookies are wonderful made with
our fresh Georgia pecans!*

1 c. butter, softened
1 c. sugar
3-oz. pkg. cream cheese,
   softened
1 egg, separated

1 T. lemon juice
1 t. vanilla extract
1/4 t. salt
2-1/4 c. all-purpose flour
2 c. pecans, finely chopped

Combine butter, sugar, cream cheese, egg yolk, lemon juice, vanilla and salt. Mix well with an electric mixer on medium speed; beat in flour. Wrap in plastic wrap; chill for at least one hour. Form into one-inch balls. In a small bowl, beat egg white lightly. Dip balls into egg white; roll in pecans. Place 2 inches apart on ungreased baking sheets. Press thumb deeply into center of each cookie. Spoon Lemon Cheese Filling into indents. Bake at 375 degrees for 10 minutes, or until filling is set. Cool slightly; remove to a wire rack. Keep refrigerated in an airtight container. Makes 6 dozen.

Lemon Cheese Filling:

3-oz. pkg. cream cheese,
   softened
1 egg yolk

1 drop yellow food coloring
1/4 c. sugar
1 T. lemon juice

Beat together all ingredients until smooth.

Connie's Orange Cookies

Lynn Walter
Winston-Salem, NC

When I was growing up, my parents and my aunt and uncle would take my brothers and my cousins on picnics together. I have such fond memories of Aunt Connie bringing along these cookies...they're my favorite!

2/3 c. shortening	2 c. all-purpose flour
3/4 c. sugar	1/2 t. baking powder
1 egg, beaten	1/2 t. baking soda
1/2 c. orange juice	1/2 t. salt

Mix together shortening, sugar and egg until well blended; stir in orange juice. In a separate bowl, combine remaining ingredients. Gradually add to shortening mixture. Drop by teaspoonfuls onto ungreased baking sheets. Bake at 400 degrees for 8 to 10 minutes. Cool and frost with Orange Frosting. Makes 3 to 4 dozen.

Orange Frosting:

2 T. butter, softened
1-1/2 c. powdered sugar

1-1/2 to 2 T. orange juice

Combine all ingredients; beat until smooth.

Tuck a packet of Connie's Orange Cookies into a pretty gift basket of breakfast foods like spiced tea, jams & jellies...so thoughtful for welcoming a new neighbor.

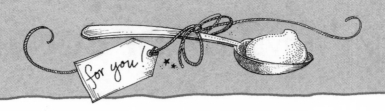

Eggnog Cookies

Kathy Baldauf
Avon, OH

Sprinkle a little nutmeg over the frosting if you like.

1 c. butter, softened
1 c. sugar
1 c. eggnog
1 egg, beaten
3-1/2 to 4 c. all-purpose flour

1 t. baking powder
1 t. baking soda
1/2 t. salt
Optional: 1/2 t. nutmeg

Mix together butter, sugar, eggnog and egg. Add flour, baking powder, baking soda, salt and nutmeg, if desired. Chill for one to 2 hours, until easy to handle. Drop by tablespoonfuls onto greased baking sheets. Bake at 350 degrees for about 8 minutes; cool. Frost cookies with Eggnog Frosting when cooled. Keep refrigerated. Makes about 5-1/2 dozen.

Eggnog Frosting:

1-1/2 c. powdered sugar

1/4 to 1/2 c. eggnog

Combine powdered sugar and 1/4 cup eggnog. Add additional eggnog as needed to reach a spreading consistency.

Add sparkle to a holiday cookie tray...simply stir some edible glitter into powdered sugar before rolling balls of drop cookie dough.

New Year's Cookies

Rebecca Boese
Alberta, Canada

So good! My grandma always made these
yummy fried treats for New Year's Day.

1 c. milk
2 T. active dry yeast
1/4 c. butter, softened
1/3 c. sugar
1-1/2 c. raisins
1 egg, beaten

2 t. lemon zest
1 t. lemon juice
1/4 t. nutmeg
3-1/2 c. all-purpose flour
oil for deep frying
Garnish: powdered sugar

Heat milk until very warm, about 110 to 115 degrees; cool to lukewarm. Add yeast; stir to dissolve. Mix in remaining ingredients except oil and powdered sugar. Knead until smooth and elastic. Cover; let rise until double in bulk. Drop into hot oil by tablespoonfuls; fry until golden, about 2 to 5 minutes. Drain on paper towels and roll in powdered sugar. Makes 2-1/2 dozen.

For a touch of whimsy, slip a gift bag of New Year's Cookies
into a festive paper party hat.

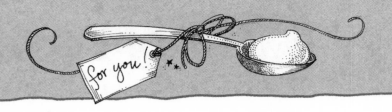

Peanut Butter Cookies

Lois Bivens
Gooseberry Patch

Everybody's lunchbox favorite!

1 c. shortening
1 c. sugar
1 c. brown sugar, packed
2 eggs, beaten

1 c. creamy peanut butter
3 c. all-purpose flour
2 t. baking soda
1 t. vanilla extract

Mix together shortening and sugars until light and fluffy. Add eggs and peanut butter, mixing well; set aside. Combine flour and baking soda; gradually add to peanut butter mixture. Stir in vanilla; mix well. Form into one-inch balls; place on ungreased baking sheets. Flatten with a floured fork in a criss-cross pattern. Bake at 350 degrees for 12 to 15 minutes. Makes about 5 dozen.

It is good to be children sometimes, and
never better than at Christmas.

-Charles Dickens

Butterscotch Chippers

Kelly Alderson
Erie, PA

People are surprised when I tell them the secret ingredient is potato chips...but not as surprised as we were, the time that Mom used barbecue potato chips by mistake!

1 c. butter, softened
1 c. brown sugar, packed
1 c. sugar
2 eggs, beaten

2-1/2 c. all-purpose flour
1 t. baking soda
1-1/3 c. butterscotch chips
2 c. potato chips, crushed

Mix together butter and sugars in a large bowl. Beat in eggs, flour and baking soda; mix well. Fold in butterscotch chips and potato chips. Drop by rounded teaspoonfuls onto lightly greased baking sheets. Bake at 350 degrees for 8 to 10 minutes. Makes 2 dozen.

Cover an empty potato chip canister with white paper, spiral
a red ribbon around it and fasten at both ends. Stack
Butterscotch Chippers inside...how clever!

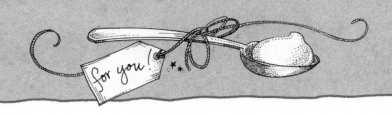

Frosted Cranberry Drops

Kendall Hale
Lynn, MA

At Christmas, I make sure to tuck a few bags of fresh cranberries into the freezer, so that we can enjoy these tasty cookies year 'round.

1/2 c. butter, softened
1 c. sugar
3/4 c. brown sugar, packed
1/4 c. milk
1 egg, beaten
2 T. orange juice

3 c. all-purpose flour
1 t. baking powder
1/4 t. baking soda
1/2 t. salt
2-1/2 c. cranberries, chopped
1 c. chopped walnuts

Blend together butter and sugars in a large bowl. Add milk, egg and orange juice; mix well. In a separate bowl, combine flour, baking powder, baking soda and salt; add to butter mixture, mixing well. Stir in berries and nuts. Drop by tablespoonfuls onto greased baking sheets. Bake at 350 degrees for 12 to 15 minutes, until golden. Cool on wire racks. Spread cookies with Powdered Sugar Frosting. Makes about 2-1/2 dozen.

Powdered Sugar Frosting:

1/3 c. butter
2 c. powdered sugar

1-1/2 t. vanilla extract
2 T. hot water

Melt butter in a saucepan over low heat until golden, about 5 minutes. Cool for 2 minutes; remove from heat. Add powdered sugar and vanilla. Beat in hot water, one tablespoon at a time, to desired consistency.

Cherry Snowballs

Shelley Turner
Boise, ID

My great-grandmother always had a plate of these crunchy cookies with the maraschino cherry surprise inside whenever I came to visit. Best of all, she'd save the cherry juice to make sweet pink milk for me!

1 c. butter, softened
2-1/2 c. powdered sugar, divided
1 T. water
1 t. vanilla extract
2 c. all-purpose flour
1 c. quick-cooking oats, uncooked

1/2 t. salt
36 maraschino cherries, patted dry
1/4 c. milk
2 c. sweetened flaked coconut

Combine butter, 1/2 cup powdered sugar, water and vanilla; set aside. In a separate bowl, mix together flour, oats and salt; gradually add to butter mixture. Shape one tablespoon dough around each cherry, forming a ball. Place 2 inches apart on ungreased baking sheets. Bake at 350 degrees for 18 to 20 minutes, until golden. Cool on wire racks. Combine remaining powdered sugar and enough milk to make a smooth frosting consistency. Dip cookies in frosting; roll in coconut. Makes 3 dozen.

Make crinkled gift basket filler in a jiffy with a paper shredder. Simply run brightly colored tissue paper or even odds & ends of printed wrapping paper through the shredder...ready to nestle in baskets and gift bags!

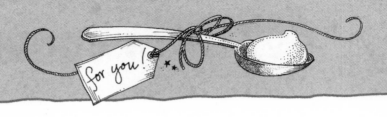

Amaretti Cookies

Kay Marone
Des Moines, IA

Light and puffy...perfect paired with after-dinner coffee!

1-1/4 c. whole blanched
   almonds
3/4 c. sugar, divided
2 egg whites, at room
   temperature

1/4 t. cream of tartar
1/4 t. almond extract
1/4 c. slivered almonds

Grind almonds and 1/4 cup sugar in a food processor until finely ground; set aside. With an electric mixer on medium speed, beat egg whites, cream of tartar and almond extract until soft peaks form. Gradually add remaining sugar, one tablespoon at a time, beating on high until very stiff peaks form and sugar is nearly dissolved. Fold in ground almonds. Drop by rounded teaspoonfuls 2 inches apart on parchment paper-lined baking sheets. Top each cookie with several slivered almonds. Bake at 300 degrees for 12 to 15 minutes, until cookies are lightly golden. Turn off oven; let cookies stand in oven with door closed for 30 minutes. Remove cookies from paper. Store in an airtight container for up to one week. Makes about 3-1/2 dozen.

Take-out containers are ideal for filling with homemade treats...
just tie with a colorful ribbon and they're ready in a jiffy!

Maple-Walnut Drops

Ann Heavey
Bridgewater, MA

Nutty for walnuts? Press a walnut half onto
each cookie before baking.

2-1/4 c. all-purpose flour
1 t. baking soda
1 t. salt
1 c. butter, softened
3/4 c. sugar

3/4 c. brown sugar, packed
1-1/2 t. maple flavoring
2 eggs, beaten
1-1/2 c. chopped walnuts

Combine flour, baking soda and salt in a small bowl; set aside. In a separate bowl, blend butter, sugars and flavoring until creamy; beat in eggs. Gradually stir in flour mixture; mix in walnuts. Drop by rounded tablespoonfuls 1-1/2 inches apart onto ungreased baking sheets. Bake at 375 degrees for 9 to 11 minutes. Makes about 4 dozen.

Stack 4 or 5 cookies and wrap in plastic wrap. Tie with curling ribbon and tuck in a sprig of holly for a tasty take-home treat to set on each guest's dinner plate.

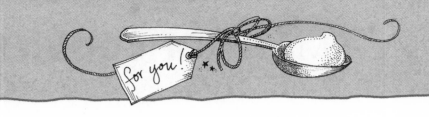

Raspberry Shortbread Thumbprints
Jennifer Wade
Long Beach, NJ

*My future mother-in-law, Kathi Baxter, kindly made me a
wonderful basket for Christmas, full of holiday goodies
including some of these yummy cookies. I love her for it!*

1 c. butter, softened
2/3 c. sugar
2 t. almond extract, divided
2 c. all-purpose flour

1/2 c. raspberry jam
1 c. powdered sugar
2 to 3 t. water

Combine butter, sugar and 1/2 teaspoon extract. Beat with an electric
mixer on medium speed until creamy, 2 to 3 minutes. Reduce speed
to low. Add flour; beat until well mixed. Cover and chill dough for at
least one hour. Form into one-inch balls. Place 2 inches apart on
ungreased baking sheets. With thumb, indent the center of each
cookie. Fill each indentation with 1/4 teaspoon jam. Bake at
350 degrees for 14 to 16 minutes, until edges are golden. Let stand
for one minute; remove from baking sheets and cool completely.
Whisk together powdered sugar, water and remaining extract until
smooth. Drizzle over cooled cookies. Makes 4 dozen.

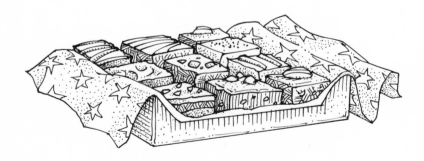

Pick up a roll of plastic food wrap in festive holiday tints...
it's the easiest-ever way to dress up a gift plate of cookies!

Coconut-Pineapple Drops

Vicki Sherry
Covington, OH

*Grandmother Clouse was a wonderful cook. These cookies are
very moist...placing wax paper between the layers
helps keep them from sticking together.*

3-1/4 c. all-purpose flour
2 t. baking powder
1 t. baking soda
1/2 t. salt
1 c. shortening

1-1/2 c. sugar
3 eggs, beaten
1 c. sweetened flaked coconut
1 c. crushed pineapple

Mix together all ingredients until well blended. Drop by teaspoonfuls
onto greased baking sheets. Bake at 350 degrees for 10 to
12 minutes. Makes 2 dozen.

Deliver a tray of cookies along with a quart of cold milk and a copy
of a favorite holiday story to a friend with little ones...what a
nice way for them to enjoy some holiday time together.

Oatmeal-Cherry Toffee Bites

Karen Buckner
Beaumont, TX

Chewy oats, cherries, crunchy toffee...what could be better?

1 c. butter, softened
1 c. brown sugar, packed
1/2 c. sugar
2 eggs
1 t. vanilla extract
1-1/2 c. all-purpose flour

1 t. baking soda
1 t. cinnamon
3 c. long-cooking oats, uncooked
1 c. dried cherries
1 c. toffee baking bits

Mix together butter and sugars. Beat in eggs, one at a time; stir in vanilla and set aside. In a separate bowl, combine flour, baking soda and cinnamon; stir into butter mixture. Stir in oats, cherries and toffee bits. Drop by rounded teaspoonfuls onto lightly greased baking sheets. Bake at 350 degrees for 8 to 10 minutes. Cool cookies on baking sheets for 5 minutes; remove to a wire rack. Makes 4 dozen.

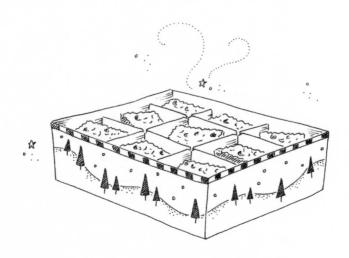

Send a Christmas cookie party in a box! When wrapping up gift boxes of homebaked cookies, why not tuck in a packet of paper holiday napkins and a box of spiced tea?

Chocolate-Covered Cherry Cookies

Carla Powers
Montevideo, MN

These are a family favorite at Christmastime.

1-1/2 c. all-purpose flour
1/2 c. baking cocoa
1/4 t. baking powder
1/4 t. baking soda
1/4 t. salt
1/2 c. butter, softened

1 c. sugar
1 egg, beaten
1-1/2 t. vanilla extract
48 maraschino cherries, patted
    dry

Blend together first 5 ingredients; set aside. In a separate bowl, blend together butter and sugar until fluffy; beat in egg and vanilla. Gradually add flour mixture to butter mixture; mix well. Form into one-inch balls; place on ungreased baking sheets. Press a cherry halfway into each ball; spoon one teaspoon Chocolate Frosting over each cherry. Bake at 350 degrees for 10 to 12 minutes. Cool on wire racks. Makes 4 dozen.

Chocolate Frosting:

6-oz. pkg. semi-sweet chocolate
    chips
1/2 c. sweetened condensed
    milk

1 to 4 t. maraschino cherry juice

Combine chocolate chips and condensed milk in a saucepan; melt over low heat, stirring constantly. Remove from heat; stir in cherry juice by teaspoonfuls until smooth.

Nestle cookies in paper cupcake liners and arrange in a
shallow box for a pretty buffet table presentation.

Lacy Florentine Cookies

Regina Vining
Warwick, RI

Sweet, buttery cookies like my Italian grandmother used to make.

3/4 c. quick-cooking oats,
    uncooked
3/4 c. all-purpose flour
3/4 c. sugar
1/2 t. baking soda
1/2 t. salt
1 t. cinnamon

1-1/2 c. sliced almonds
10 T. butter, melted
1/4 c. half-and-half
1/4 c. light corn syrup
1 t. vanilla extract
4 1-oz. sqs. semi-sweet baking
    chocolate, melted

Whisk together oats, flour, sugar, baking soda, salt and cinnamon; add almonds. Stir in butter, half-and-half, corn syrup and vanilla until well combined. Drop by heaping teaspoonfuls 3 inches apart onto aluminum foil-lined, greased baking sheets, 6 cookies per sheet. Bake at 350 degrees on center rack, one sheet at a time, until edges are golden, 7 to 9 minutes. Cool for several minutes; transfer to a wire rack. Drizzle melted chocolate over cookies. Makes 4 dozen.

Give a gift of a family movie night! Decorate a new paint pail with Christmas cut-outs, then tuck in a classic holiday movie, microwave popcorn and some of your yummiest homemade cookies. They'll love it!

Sweet Cinna-Ginger Cookies

Laura Fuller
Fort Wayne, IN

No one should have to miss out on cookies at Christmas!
My father-in-law can't have sugar, so I found
this yummy cookie recipe for him.

6 T. shortening
6 T. margarine, softened
1 c. powdered calorie-free
    sweetener
1 egg, beaten

1/4 c. molasses
2 c. all-purpose flour
1 t. cinnamon
3/4 t. ground ginger
1/2 t. ground cloves

Combine shortening, margarine, sweetener, egg and molasses. In a separate bowl, mix remaining ingredients and add to shortening mixture; blend thoroughly. Chill until firm, about 2 hours. Form by tablespoonfuls into 30 balls. Arrange on ungreased baking sheets; press down gently with a fork to make a criss-cross pattern. Bake at 350 degrees for 10 to 12 minutes; do not overbake. Cool on a wire rack. Makes about 2-1/2 dozen.

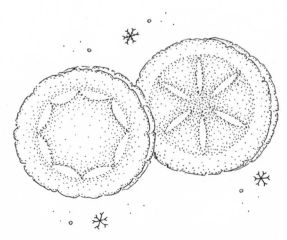

Check your cupboard for glass tumblers with pretty patterns
on the bottom. Just dip the glass in sugar and press
to flatten walnut-size balls of dough.

39

Banana Drop Cookies

Jackie Lewelling
Reno, NV

This was my mother's best cookie recipe. Everyone in the family loved the cookies, and of course, they always asked for the recipe.

2/3 c. shortening
1-3/4 c. sugar, divided
1 t. vanilla extract
2 eggs, beaten
1 c. ripe banana, mashed

2-1/4 c. all-purpose flour
2 t. baking powder
1/4 t. salt
1 c. chopped nuts
1/2 t. cinnamon

Blend shortening, 1-1/2 cups sugar and vanilla until light and fluffy. Add eggs and beat well; stir in mashed banana. Stir in flour, baking powder, salt and nuts; mix well. Chill for 30 minutes to overnight. Drop by teaspoonfuls onto greased baking sheets. Mix remaining sugar and cinnamon together; sprinkle on unbaked cookies. Bake at 400 degrees for 8 to 10 minutes. Makes 3 dozen.

For a quick & easy goodie bag, cut colorful construction paper the same width as a plastic zipping bag...fold in half and decorate. Staple on top of bag.

Rudolph's Carrot Cookies

Diana Cunningham
Lafayette, LA

Top with cream cheese frosting for an extra-special touch.

1/2 c. shortening
1/2 c. butter, softened
1 c. brown sugar, packed
1 c. sugar
2 eggs
1 t. vanilla extract
1 c. carrots, peeled and finely
   shredded

1 c. chopped walnuts
Optional: 1/2 c. sweetened
   flaked coconut
2-1/2 c. all-purpose flour
1 t. baking powder
1 t. baking soda
1 t. salt

Blend shortening and butter in a large bowl. Add sugars, mixing well. Beat in eggs, one at a time; add vanilla. Stir in carrots, walnuts and coconut, if desired; set aside. In a separate bowl, mix together remaining ingredients. Gradually add to shortening mixture until well blended; chill for one hour. Drop by tablespoonfuls 2 inches apart onto greased baking sheets. Bake at 350 degrees for 8 to 10 minutes, until golden. Makes 4 dozen.

Grandma always says, "Never return a dish empty." Christmas is a perfect time to gather up casserole dishes and pie plates that have been left behind, fill with homebaked goodies and return to their owners!

Cocoa Gobs

Billie Jean Elliott
Woodsfield, OH

Every Christmas, when our children were young, we spent many hours baking cookies to share with friends & neighbors. One of our favorites was called a Gob...they are delicious! Now our children are grown and married with children of their own, and they all love Gobs too.

1/2 c. shortening
2 c. sugar
2 eggs, beaten
1 c. buttermilk
3/4 c. boiling water
1 t. vanilla extract

4 c. all-purpose flour
1/2 c. baking cocoa
2 t. baking soda
1/2 t. baking powder
1/2 t. salt
Garnish: powdered sugar

Blend together shortening, sugar and eggs. Add buttermilk, boiling water and vanilla; set aside. In a separate bowl, mix together flour, cocoa, baking soda, baking powder and salt; gradually add to shortening mixture. Drop by rounded teaspoonfuls onto ungreased baking sheets. Bake at 450 degrees for 5 minutes; cool. Assemble cookies in pairs with filling in between; sprinkle powdered sugar over tops and bottoms of cookies. Makes about 2 dozen.

Filling:

1 c. milk
5 T. all-purpose flour
1/2 c. butter, softened
1/2 c. shortening

1 c. powdered sugar
1 t. vanilla extract
1/4 t. salt

Combine milk and flour in a saucepan over medium heat, stirring constantly, until thickened. Cool. Blend remaining ingredients. Stir milk mixture into butter mixture until consistency of whipped icing.

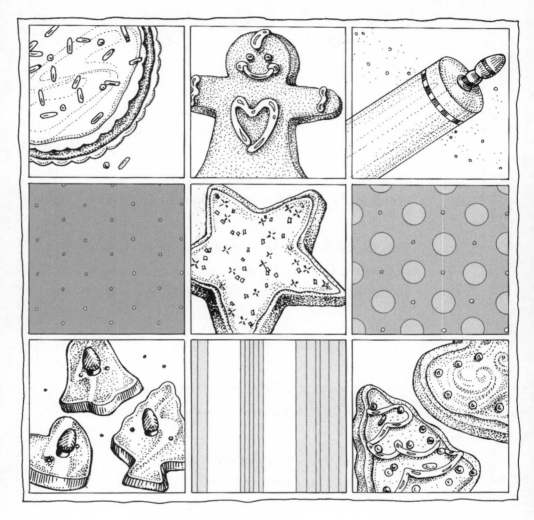

Clever
CUT-OUTS

Baking with Kids

Share the delight of Christmas baking with children for
memories in the making! Cut-out cookies are a great choice
for budding bakers, with lots of fun shapes to choose
from and brightly colored sweet trimmings galore.

° ❄ °

Even the smallest children can pick out their favorite
cookie cutters. Little ones love to pretend they're cooking,
so keep some unbreakable plastic measuring spoons,
cups and bowls handy.

° ❄ °

Older kids can measure out ingredients and mix up dough.
They can even write out recipes and draw illustrations
to make their very own keepsake recipe books.

° ❄ °

Why not host a kids' cookie decorating party...
invite moms too! Before party day, bake up lots
of sugar cookie Santas, angels, reindeer, snowmen
and gingerbread boys. Set out bowls of frosting and
candy sprinkles...just let imaginations take over!

Clever CUT-OUTS

Spicy Molasses Cookies

Ruby Webb
Haywarden, IA

*As soon as we smell the first batch of these spicy cookies baking
in the oven, we know Christmas is coming!*

1 c. butter, softened
1/2 c. sugar
1/2 c. brown sugar, packed
1/2 c. molasses
2/3 c. light corn syrup
4-1/2 c. all-purpose flour

1 t. baking soda
1 t. salt
1 t. ground ginger
1 t. ground cloves
1 t. cinnamon
Garnish: frosting

Blend butter and sugars together. Add molasses and corn syrup; mix
well. Combine dry ingredients and add to butter mixture; knead until
smooth. Chill for several hours, until firm. On a lightly floured surface,
roll out to less than 1/8-inch thick. Cut with floured cookie cutters and
place on lightly greased baking sheets. Bake at 350 degrees for
8 minutes. Cool on a wire rack; decorate with frosting as desired.
Makes 4 to 5 dozen.

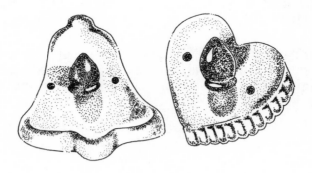

Here's an easy trick to help cut-out cookie shapes bake up neatly.
Place cookies on a parchment paper-lined baking sheet and
pop into the fridge for 10 to 15 minutes, then bake.

45

Grandma Mary's Shortbread

Kerry McNeil
Anacortes, WA

I received this wonderful recipe 20 years ago from a dear friend who was like a grandmother to me. When my husband and I owned a bakery, we used it every spring to bake pink, yellow and violet frosted tulip cookies by the thousands for our county's annual tulip festival.

1 c. butter, softened	1/2 c. superfine sugar
2 c. all-purpose flour	2 T. cornstarch

Combine all ingredients in a medium bowl and knead to form a smooth dough. Roll out on a floured surface to 1/4-inch thick. Cut out with a cookie or biscuit cutter. Transfer to ungreased baking sheets. Bake at 275 degrees for 45 minutes; cool. Frost with Cream Cheese Frosting. Refrigerate until set or ready to serve. Makes 2-1/2 dozen.

Cream Cheese Frosting:

8-oz. pkg. cream cheese, softened	16-oz. pkg. powdered sugar
1/2 c. butter, softened	Optional: few drops food coloring
2 t. vanilla extract	

With an electric mixer on medium speed, beat cream cheese and butter together. Add vanilla and mix well. On low speed, add powdered sugar until mixed. Beat on high speed for one minute. Tint with food coloring, if desired.

Tie on a cookie cutter with colored jute...a quick & easy package decoration.

$\mathcal{C}$lever **CUT-OUTS**

Brown Sugar Shortbread Cookies
Renee Velderman
Hopkins, MI

These simple cookies are a big favorite in our house. In fact, most of the time, I have to double the recipe so that they will last through the day. I made these for a ladies' holiday gathering at church using a star-shaped cookie cutter...everyone loved them!

1 c. butter, softened
1/2 c. brown sugar, packed

2-1/4 c. all-purpose flour

Blend together butter and sugar; gradually stir in flour. Turn onto a lightly floured surface and knead until smooth. Pat into an 11"x8" rectangle about 1/3-inch thick; cut into 2-inch by 1-inch strips. Arrange on ungreased baking sheets one inch apart. Pierce surface with a fork. Bake at 300 degrees for 25 minutes, or until beginning to turn golden on bottom. Cool for 5 minutes; remove to a wire rack to cool completely. Makes 3-1/2 dozen.

Bake up some sugar cookie ornaments for old-fashioned charm on the Christmas tree. Cut out cookie dough and make a small hole at the top of each unbaked cookie with a drinking straw. After baking, thread a ribbon through the hole for hanging.

Maple Sugar Cookies

Michelle Crabtree
Lee's Summit, MO

Use only pure maple syrup for the yummiest flavor.

1 c. butter-flavored shortening	3 c. all-purpose flour
1-1/4 c. sugar	3/4 t. baking powder
2 eggs	1/2 t. baking soda
1/4 c. maple syrup	1/2 t. salt
1 T. vanilla extract	

Blend together shortening and sugar. Add eggs, one at a time, beating well after each addition. Beat in syrup and vanilla. In a separate bowl, combine remaining ingredients; gradually add to shortening mixture. Cover and refrigerate for 2 hours, or until easy to handle. On a lightly floured surface, roll out to 1/8-inch thick. Cut with a 2-1/2 inch cookie cutter dipped in flour. Arrange on ungreased baking sheets one inch apart. Bake at 375 degrees for 8 to 10 minutes, until golden. Remove to wire rack; cool. Makes 2 dozen.

Take two gift bags of the same size but different colors. Cut through the middle of each, swap halves and glue together, overlapping edges by 1/2 inch. Glue a strip of wide ribbon around each bag to hide the seam...voilà, two clever boutique bags for giving cookies!

Cake Mix Cut-Outs

Terri White
Catlettsburg, KY

*These are so easy to make, you'll want to mix up several
batches using different flavors of cake mix!*

18-1/2 oz. pkg. yellow cake mix
1/2 c. butter, softened
1 t. vanilla extract

2 eggs, beaten
Garnish: frosting

Combine all ingredients except frosting; mix until smooth. Roll dough
out on a floured surface to 1/4-inch thick; cut into desired shapes with
cookie cutters. Place on ungreased baking sheets. Bake at 350 degrees
for 12 to 15 minutes, until tops are lightly golden and edges are done.
Cool; frost as desired. Makes about 3 dozen.

Mix up some egg yolk paint...kids can really let their creativity shine!
For each color, beat an egg yolk until smooth, then stir in 5 to
6 drops of food coloring. Give kids a clean new paintbrush
to paint unbaked cookies, then bake as usual.

Mom's Sour Cream Cookies

Karen McCann
Marion, OH

Many years ago, my mother made these cut-outs a family tradition. We would all cut out our favorite shapes and frost the cookies to our liking. I have since passed that on to my daughter, Stacy, and she has now carried on that tradition with their children.

1 c. butter, softened
1 t. baking powder
1-1/2 c. sugar
2 eggs, beaten
1 c. sour cream

1-1/2 t. vanilla extract
4-1/2 c. all-purpose flour
1 t. salt
1/2 t. nutmeg

Blend together butter and baking powder; add sugar, eggs, sour cream and vanilla. Combine remaining ingredients; gradually add to butter mixture. Knead on a floured surface. Roll out to 1/4-inch thick and cut out with cookie cutters. Transfer to lightly greased baking sheets. Bake at 350 degrees for 15 to 20 minutes, until golden; cool. Spread cookies with frosting. Makes about 5 dozen.

Frosting:

1 c. powdered sugar
1 T. milk

1/2 t. vanilla extract
few drops food coloring

Mix all ingredients together until creamy.

50

$\mathcal{C}$lever **CUT-OUTS**

Granny Hodge's Teacakes

Julie Marsh
Shelbyville, TN

My Granny Hodge gave me a copy of this recipe when I was young and starting my own recipe collection. Years later, after Granny had passed away, my aunt gave me a copy of Granny's same hand-written recipe with a little note, "Mama used to make these for us all when we were kids." I always think of my Mom and Granny Hodge while making these cookies at Christmastime for my family.

2-1/4 c. sugar, divided
3 eggs, beaten
5 c. all-purpose flour
2 T. buttermilk

1 c. butter, softened
1 t. baking soda
1 t. vanilla extract

Mix together 2 cups sugar and remaining ingredients. Roll out on a floured surface to 1/8-inch thick. Cut with favorite Christmas cookie cutters. Sprinkle lightly with reserved sugar. Transfer to lightly greased baking sheets. Bake at 400 degrees for 10 to 12 minutes, until golden. Makes 2 dozen.

Add a little variety to plain sugar cookie dough!
Try using other flavoring extracts instead of vanilla.
Almond, peppermint and lemon are all delightful.

Pistachio-Lime Cookies

Tina Wright
Atlanta, GA

For a shiny glazed finish, beat an egg white until frothy. Brush
it over unbaked cookies, sprinkle with sugar and bake.

1 c. butter, softened	2 c. all-purpose flour
1 c. sugar	1 t. lime zest
1 egg, beaten	1 c. pistachios, finely chopped

Beat together butter and sugar; add egg. Stir in flour and lime zest; add pistachios and mix well. Cover and chill for one hour. Roll dough out on a floured surface to 1/4-inch thick; cut with cookie cutters. Place on ungreased baking sheets. Bake at 375 degrees for 8 to 10 minutes, until lightly golden; cool. Pipe Lime Icing around cookies to outline. Makes about 1-1/2 dozen.

Lime Icing:

2 T. butter, softened	1 T. milk
1 c. powdered sugar	1/4 t. lime zest

Beat together all ingredients until smooth.

Spell out names on gift tags with simple letter stamps
or stickers to give gifts a creative touch.

Lemon Tea Cookies

Anna McMaster
Portland, OR

Refreshing lemony sugar cookies you'll love with hot tea.

3/4 c. butter, melted
1-1/4 c. sugar
1/4 t. lemon extract
2 eggs, beaten

3-1/4 c. all-purpose flour
1/2 t. baking soda
1/8 t. salt
Garnish: additional sugar

Combine butter, sugar and extract; beat in eggs. In a separate bowl, mix together flour, baking soda and salt; gradually add to butter mixture. Roll out onto a lightly floured surface, about 1/8-inch thick. Cut with a round or shaped cookie cutter and place on lightly greased baking sheets, one inch apart. Sprinkle lightly with sugar. Bake at 375 degrees for 10 to 12 minutes, until golden. Makes 4 to 5 dozen.

Turn Lemon Tea Cookies into yummy sandwich cookies! Before baking, use a mini heart or star cutter to cut out the centers of half of the cookies. Sandwich cooled cookies in pairs with lemon curd or vanilla frosting in between.

Snowflake Crunch Mix

Cricket Heffron
West Jordan, UT

I started out making this chocolatey snack mix just for the kids, but adults really gobble it up too! It looks like a bag of snowflakes. I like to fill pretty cello bags or clear jars and tie them with ribbon or raffia.

1/2 c. margarine
1 c. creamy peanut butter
12-oz. pkg. semi-sweet
   chocolate chips

12-oz. pkg. corn & rice cereal
3 c. powdered sugar

Melt margarine, peanut butter and chocolate chips together in a saucepan over low heat, stirring constantly, until well blended. Remove from heat. Place cereal into a large bowl and pour chocolate mixture over top; mix thoroughly. Pour powdered sugar into a large brown paper bag. Add cereal mixture; gently shake to evenly coat. Let cool; place in airtight containers. Makes 10 to 12 cups.

Dress up an empty coffee can for giving Snowflake Crunch Mix. Simply cut a strip of icy blue scrapbooking paper to fit around the can and tape ends together. Decorate by gluing on foam snowflake cut-outs or colorful buttons.

Snowman Crispy Pops

Amy Butcher
Columbus, GA

These make wonderful school gifts. One year we got so carried away with decorating that we gave the snowmen little hats made of mint wafers topped with mini peanut butter cups...such fun!

1/2 c. butter
2 10-oz. pkgs. marshmallows
12 c. crispy rice cereal
10 to 12 wooden skewers

8 1-oz. sqs. white baking chocolate, chopped
Garnish: assorted small candies, broken pretzels, fruit leather

Place butter in a large microwave-safe bowl. Microwave on high setting for about 1-1/2 minutes, stirring every 30 seconds. Add marshmallows; microwave on high setting for 3 minutes, stirring every minute until melted. Stir in cereal. With buttered hands, pat mixture into an aluminum foil-lined, greased 15"x10" jelly-roll pan. Chill for 30 minutes, or until firm. Cut out circles using 3-inch round cookie cutters. For each snowman pop, insert a skewer through 3 circles; set aside. Microwave chocolate on high setting for one to 1-1/2 minutes until melted; stir until smooth. Spoon melted chocolate over pops to coat. Decorate as desired with small candies, using broken pretzels for arms and strips of fruit leather for scarves. Place on a wire rack until set. Makes 10 to 12.

Make sure to have lots of extra chocolate chips, nuts and other cookie-baking goodies for sneaking, especially if you have little helpers lending a hand!

Grandma Erna's Molasses Cookies

Lisa Wohlhuter
Welcome, MN

My husband's grandma taught me how to make these molasses cookies with their marshmallowy frosting. They are a family favorite and are a big hit at church bake sales too.

2 c. brown sugar, packed
1-1/2 c. margarine, softened
1 c. molasses
1/2 c. boiling water
1 T. baking soda
1 t. salt

1 t. cinnamon
1 t. ground ginger
1/2 t. nutmeg
1/2 t. ground cloves
6 c. all-purpose flour

Combine all ingredients in a large bowl; mix until very stiff. Refrigerate for several hours or overnight. Roll out onto a floured surface to 1/4-inch thick. Cut out with a 3-inch round cookie cutter; place on ungreased baking sheets. Bake at 350 degrees for 8 to 10 minutes; cool. Spread cookies with Creamy White Frosting and let dry. Makes 10 to 12 dozen.

Creamy White Frosting:

1-1/2 c. sugar
1/2 c. water
1 t. vinegar

1 c. mini marshmallows
2 pasteurized egg whites

Combine sugar, water and vinegar in a heavy saucepan over medium-high heat; cover and bring to a boil. Uncover; cook until mixture reaches the soft-ball stage, or 234 to 243 degrees on a candy thermometer; remove from heat. Stir in marshmallows until melted. Beat egg whites until frothy; gradually add marshmallow mixture. With an electric mixer, beat on high speed until semi-stiff peaks form.

Gingerbread Men

Carol Tumbarello
Bentonville, VA

Go ahead and nibble on the dough!
It's OK, there are no eggs in it.

1 c. butter, softened
1 c. sugar
1 c. molasses
2 T. ground ginger
Optional: 1/4 c. crystallized
   ginger, finely chopped

1 t. baking soda
1 t. salt
5 c. all-purpose flour, divided

Blend together butter, sugar and molasses. Stir in ginger and crystal-lized ginger, if using. In a large bowl, combine baking soda, salt and one cup flour; add to butter mixture. Stir in remaining flour, 1/4 cup at a time, and knead by hand as it becomes stiff. Knead until well blended. Roll out onto a lightly floured surface to about 1/4-inch thick. Cut out desired shapes and arrange on parchment paper-lined baking sheets. Bake at 350 degrees for 8 to 10 minutes. Makes 4 to 5 dozen.

A cookie baking kit that any busy mom would love to receive! Mix up
a batch of your favorite cookie dough, wrap in plastic wrap and freeze.
Tuck it into a big mixing bowl along with cookie cutters, tubs
of frosting, sprinkles and a copy of the recipe. So thoughtful!

Low-Sugar Cut-Outs

Virginia Watson
Scranton, PA

My kids love to draw on these cookies with food coloring marker pens.
It's a fun way to decorate them without adding sugar.

1 c. butter, softened
1 c. powdered low-calorie sugar
   blend for baking
2 eggs
2 t. vanilla extract

4 c. all-purpose flour
1 t. baking powder
1/2 t. salt
Optional: colored sugar

With an electric mixer on medium speed, beat butter until creamy.
Gradually add sugar blend, beating well. Add eggs, one at a time,
mixing well. Stir in vanilla. In a separate bowl, combine flour,
baking powder and salt. Gradually add to butter mixture. Divide
dough in half; pat each half into a circle and wrap with plastic wrap.
Chill for one hour, until somewhat firm. Roll out 1/8-inch thick on a
lightly floured surface, one-half of dough at a time. Cut out with
cookie cutters; place on lightly greased baking sheets. Sprinkle
lightly with colored sugar, if desired. Bake at 325 degrees for 8 to
10 minutes, until lightly golden around edges. Cool slightly on baking
sheets; remove to wire racks to cool completely. Makes 2-1/2 dozen.

Don't forget friends & relatives
who can't indulge in sugary treats
at Christmas! Folks who are
diabetic or counting calories
would appreciate a plate of
low-sugar or sugar-free cookies...
tuck in some colorful sugar-free
hard candies too.

Clever CUT-OUTS

Brown Sugar Hot Tea

Megan Brooks
Antioch, TN

*My granddaughter feels so grown-up when I share a pot of this
special tea with her. I've found the brown sugar low-calorie
sweetener works well with it also.*

6 c. boiling water
6 teabags

1/2 c. brown sugar, packed
Optional: milk or cream

Pour boiling water over teabags into a teapot and cover. Steep for
5 minutes. Remove teabags and discard. Stir in brown sugar; add
a splash of milk or cream, if desired. Makes 6 servings.

Bring country charm right into the kitchen with a mini Christmas tree!
Trim it with sugar cookies, tea strainers, cookie cutters, toy-size
kitchen utensils and garlands of dried spices and apple slices.

Chocolate Mint Stars

Lisa Wagner
Gooseberry Patch

Mmm...chocolate and peppermint in every crunchy bite!

1-1/4 c. all purpose flour
1/2 c. baking cocoa
1/2 t. salt
1 c. butter, softened
1 c. powdered sugar

1 t. vanilla extract
6-oz. pkg. semi-sweet chocolate chips, chopped
1/2 c. peppermint candies, finely crushed

Combine flour, cocoa and salt. In a separate bowl, beat together butter and powdered sugar until smooth; mix in vanilla. Gradually add flour mixture to butter mixture and mix well. Divide in half and wrap in plastic wrap; chill until firm, 45 minutes to one hour. Roll out 1/4-inch thick on a floured surface, one-half at a time. Cut out with a 3-inch star-shaped cutter. Arrange one inch apart on parchment paper-lined baking sheets. Bake at 300 degrees on center oven rack, one sheet at a time, until tops feel firm, about 25 minutes. Cool on baking sheets for 10 minutes. Remove to wire racks; cool completely. Melt chocolate chips in the top of a double boiler over simmering water; stir until smooth. Drizzle chocolate over cookies; sprinkle with crushed candy. Let stand until chocolate is set, at least one hour. Store in an airtight container at room temperature. Makes 2-1/2 dozen.

Make sure frostings and toppings have set and hardened completely before packing cookies in boxes. Wax paper or parchment paper will keep layers separated.

CLeVer **CUT-OUTS**

Triple-Layer Chocolate Mints

Marilyn Miller
Fort Washington, PA

Chocolate lovers will swoon!

6 1-oz. sqs. semi-sweet baking
   chocolate, chopped
6-oz. pkg. white baking
   chocolate, chopped

1 t. peppermint extract
4 1.55-oz. milk chocolate bars,
   chopped

Line an 8"x8" baking pan with aluminum foil, leaving a one-inch overhang on sides; set aside. Place semi-sweet chocolate in top of double boiler over simmering water; stir until melted. Remove from heat; spread in pan. Let stand until firm. If not firm after 45 minutes, refrigerate for 10 minutes. Melt white chocolate in clean double boiler; stir in extract. Spread over semi-sweet chocolate. Gently shake pan to spread evenly. Let stand 45 minutes, or until set. Melt milk chocolate in clean double boiler; spread over white chocolate. Shake pan to spread evenly. Let stand 45 minutes, or until set. With aluminum foil handles, remove from pan; place on cutting board. Slice into one-inch squares. Makes 64 pieces.

A tin filled with favorite Christmas cookies and candies
is extra special when the recipes are included!

Merry Christmas Hot Punch

Mary Lyhane
Marysville, KS

Our family makes this beverage every Christmas Eve. Not only does it make the house smell wonderful, but it warms you up on a snowy evening. Everyone enjoys drinking this while the children unwrap gifts... even our little grandchildren love it!

2 64-oz. bottles tangerine juice
5 c. apple juice
2/3 c. powdered calorie-free
  sweetener

4 4-inch cinnamon sticks
1 t. cinnamon
Garnish: orange slices,
  whole cloves

Combine all ingredients except garnish in a large stockpot. Heat to boiling over medium-high heat; reduce to a simmer for 10 minutes. Serve warm, garnished with thin slices of orange, studded with whole cloves. Makes about 40 servings of 1/2 cup each.

Cookie cutters make fun travel souvenirs...they're inexpensive and don't take up much room in a suitcase. Select shapes to remind you of favorite places. Later, share happy vacation memories as you bake together.

Christmas Butter Cookies

Kimber Wagner
Cordova, TN

Every year my Grandma Wallace would make cookies and decorate them. When she developed Alzheimer's, my sisters and I started making them for our family. We have Cookie Day and have made as many as 56 dozen! It will always be a memory that brings back lots of smiles.

3/4 c. butter, softened
1 c. sugar
1 egg, beaten
2 T. evaporated milk
1 t. vanilla extract

3 c. all-purpose flour
1 t. baking powder
1/2 t. baking soda
1/2 t. salt

Blend together butter, sugar, egg, evaporated milk and vanilla; mix well. Add remaining ingredients. Roll out on a lightly floured surface to 1/4-inch thick. Cut out with cookie cutters; place on ungreased baking sheets. Bake at 350 degrees for about 10 minutes, just until golden. Makes 3 to 4 dozen.

Frost snowflake cut-out cookies with white icing and sprinkle with sparkling white sanding sugar...shimmery!

Hungarian Pecan Cookies

Laina Lamb
Bucyrus, OH

These cookies were handed down from my Dad's Hungarian grandmother and we've lost the original name for them. But no Christmas season would be complete without them. They freeze well too.

2 c. butter, softened
16-oz. container cottage cheese
4 c. all-purpose flour
2 6-oz. pkgs. pecans, finely
   ground

1/2 c. sugar
1/4 c. water
Garnish: powdered sugar

Combine butter and cottage cheese until well blended; add flour and mix well. Cover and chill for several hours, or overnight. Combine pecans, sugar and water; chill, covered for 30 minutes. Roll dough out on a lightly floured surface to 1/8-inch thick. Cut into 2-inch squares. Spoon 1/2 teaspoon pecan mixture into center of each square. Fold opposite corners over filling; press to seal. Carefully transfer to ungreased baking sheets. Bake at 375 degrees for 8 to 10 minutes, until golden. Cool on wire racks; roll carefully in powdered sugar just before serving. Makes 10 dozen.

Plastic zipping bags are oh-so handy for piping on colored frosting. Fill a small bag with frosting and seal, then snip off a tiny corner...frosting will squeeze out easily. Afterwards, just toss away the empty bag!

Iced Shortbread Cookies

Patty Kelly
Godfrey, IL

My mom found this recipe in an old cookbook when I was a little girl. It was the very first recipe that I remember baking. We would sprinkle sugar on them and then bake, but now I like to bake them without the sugar and ice them with buttercream frosting.

2/3 c. butter-flavored shortening
1-1/4 c. sugar
2 eggs, beaten
1 T. milk
1 t. vanilla extract
3 c. all-purpose flour
2 t. baking powder
1 t. salt

Blend together shortening, sugar, eggs, milk and vanilla until blended well. Gradually add flour, baking powder and salt; mix until smooth. Roll out onto a floured surface and cut into desired shapes, or cut out with a drinking glass. Transfer cookies to aluminum foil-lined baking sheets. Bake at 375 degrees for 8 to 10 minutes. Cool completely; spread with Buttercream Frosting. Makes about 3 dozen.

Buttercream Frosting:

16-oz. pkg. powdered sugar
1/4 t. salt
1/4 c. milk
1/3 c. butter, softened
Optional: assorted colors food coloring

Beat together all ingredients except food coloring until smooth. Add additional milk to reach desired consistency. Divide into separate bowls and add food coloring, if desired.

For crisp, golden cookies, group similar-size cut-outs together on baking sheets, rather than a mix of small and large shapes. They'll be much less likely to overbake.

Raisin-Filled Cookies

Barbara Schmeckpeper
Minooka, IL

My grandma loved to cook, bake and can...she did so many special things. At Christmas, she always served hot chocolate in Santa Claus mugs to us grandchildren along with these delicious cookies. What fond memories!

1 c. shortening	4 c. all-purpose flour
1 c. sugar	1 t. baking soda
1 c. brown sugar, packed	1/2 t. salt
3 eggs, beaten	1 t. vanilla extract

Mix together all ingredients until well combined. Roll out on a lightly floured surface to 1/4-inch thick. Cut out with a round cookie cutter. Spread Raisin Filling onto half the cookies. Arrange remaining cookies over filling; press edges with a fork dipped in flour to seal. Bake at 350 degrees for 9 to 10 minutes. Makes 3 dozen.

Raisin Filling:

1 c. raisins, finely chopped	1 T. sugar
1/2 c. water	1 T. all-purpose flour

Mix together all ingredients in a saucepan over medium heat. Bring to a boil. Remove from heat; cool slightly.

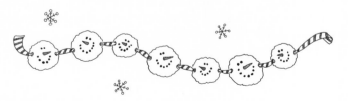

Best of all are the decorations the grandchildren have made...
fat little stars and rather crooked Santas, shaped
out of dough and baked in the oven.

-Gladys Taber

Clever CUT-OUTS

Jolly Cinna-Men

Michelle Crabtree
Lee's Summit, MO

There's such a wonderful aroma in the air when these are baking!

1 c. margarine, softened
2-1/4 c. brown sugar, packed
3 eggs, beaten

4 c. all-purpose flour
1 t. baking soda
1 t. cinnamon

Blend together margarine and brown sugar; add eggs and beat well. Add remaining ingredients; mix well and chill overnight. Divide dough in half and roll out, one portion at a time, on a floured surface to 1/4-inch thick. Keep remaining dough refrigerated until ready to roll out. If dough becomes too soft, place in freezer for a few minutes. Cut into desired shapes. Bake on a greased baking sheets at 350 degrees for 7 to 8 minutes. Makes about 1-1/2 dozen.

Kids will love their very own tasty gingerbread twins!
Personalize each gingerbread boy or girl with frosting hair,
eyes, freckles and other features...add clothing too.
They'll look so sweet peeking out of stockings.

Zesty Lemon Cut-Outs

Jill Burton
Gooseberry Patch

*I always host a Christmas tea early in December, so my best girlfriends
and I can celebrate together before the season gets too busy. I set a
pretty table with my holiday linens, holly-painted tea set, fresh red
roses and lots of homebaked cookies. Of all the cookies I've served, my
guests say they like this one best of all!*

2-1/4 c. all-purpose flour
3/4 t. cinnamon
1/4 t. allspice
1/8 t. nutmeg
1/8 t. ground cloves
1/8 t. salt
2/3 c. butter, softened

3-oz. pkg. cream cheese,
  softened
1/2 c. sugar
3 T. milk
1-1/2 t. lemon zest
Garnish: candy sprinkles

Whisk together flour, spices and salt; set aside. In a separate bowl,
with an electric mixer on medium speed, beat together butter, cream
cheese and sugar until well combined. Beat in milk and lemon zest.
Gradually add flour mixture, beating at low speed just until combined.
Chill, covered, for 2 to 3 hours. On a lightly floured surface, roll out
dough to about 1/8-inch thick. Cut out shapes with cookie cutters;
arrange on ungreased baking sheets. Bake at 350 degrees for 8 to
10 minutes, until lightly golden on bottom. Cool on wire racks. Frost
cooled cookies with Meringue Frosting; decorate with candy sprinkles.
Makes about 5 dozen.

Meringue Frosting:

2 c. powdered sugar
4 t. meringue powder

1/4 t. cream of tartar
3 T. warm water

Combine all ingredients in a medium bowl; beat with an electric mixer
on low speed until combined. Increase to medium-high speed for 7 to
10 minutes, until stiff peaks form. If too stiff, add a little more water,
1/2 teaspoon at a time. Keep covered until ready to use.

Clever CUT-OUTS

Velvety Butter Cookies

Jacqueline Kurtz
Wernersville, PA

*Rich with butter and cream cheese, these
cookies are almost decadent.*

2 c. butter, softened
8-oz. pkg. cream cheese,
   softened
2 c. sugar

2 egg yolks
1 t. vanilla extract
4-1/2 c. all-purpose flour

Combine all ingredients; mix well. Chill for 2 hours. Roll out on a
lightly floured surface to 1/4-inch thick. Cut out with cookie cutters.
Bake on greased baking sheets at 350 degrees for 10 to 12 minutes.
Makes 7 dozen.

A cookie tree...how fun! Use a graduated set of star-shaped cookie
cutters to bake up a stack of cookies. Use green frosting to decorate
and stack cookies, then decorate with tiny candies.

Christmas Medallions

Tiffany Brinkley
Broomfield, CO

*These cookies look so pretty, yet they're really very simple
to make. The little holiday-shaped inserts from my linzer
cookie cutter set work very well for this recipe, I've found.*

1 c. butter, softened
2/3 c. sugar
1 egg, beaten
1-1/2 t. almond extract
1/2 t. salt

2-1/2 c. all-purpose flour
2 T. water
2 t. pasteurized dried egg whites
Garnish: colored sanding sugar

Combine butter, sugar, egg, almond extract and salt in a large bowl.
With an electric mixer on medium speed, beat until creamy. Blend in
flour on low speed until well mixed. Divide dough in half; wrap in
plastic wrap and chill until firm, one to 2 hours. Roll out dough,
one-half at a time, to 1/4-inch thick on a floured surface. Cut out with
a 2-inch round cookie cutter; place 2 inches apart onto ungreased
baking sheets. Lightly press a mini cookie cutter into center of each
cookie; do not cut through dough. Bake at 350 degrees for 9 to
11 minutes, until lightly golden. Let stand one minute; remove from
baking sheets and cool completely. Whisk water and egg whites
together in a small bowl. With a small brush, paint mixture over
center design and rim of each cookie. Sprinkle with sanding sugar;
shake off any excess and let dry. Makes 3 dozen.

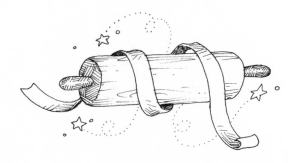

A silicone baking mat makes quick work of rolling out
cookie dough...no more sticking or tearing!

Clever CUT-OUTS

Pecan Crescent Roll-Ups

Beverly Ray
Brandon, FL

These crunchy, nutty treats are so simple to make.

1/2 c. chopped pecans
1/4 c. sugar
1/4 t. cinnamon

1 refrigerated pie crust
1 T. water

Combine pecans, sugar and cinnamon in a small bowl; set aside.
Unfold crust on a lightly floured surface; roll out into a 12-inch circle.
Brush crust with water; spread nut mixture over crust. With a pizza
cutter, divide circle into 16 wedge-shaped slices. Roll up wedges to
form crescents, starting at outer edge of each slice. Place on lightly
greased baking sheets one inch apart. Bake at 375 degrees for 20 to
25 minutes, until golden. Makes about 16.

Make your own colored sugar...it's easy! Combine 1/2 cup sugar and 5 to
7 drops food coloring in a small lidded jar. Close jar and shake until
sugar is evenly tinted. Spread sugar on a baking sheet to dry.

Buttermilk Sugar Cookies

Laina Lamb
Bucyrus, OH

This is my mom's grandmother's cookie recipe. The cookies are soft as silk, but hold up to being cut out and frosted. I've made side-by-side comparisons with lots of other sugar cookies, and none come close to Grandma's...Christmas wouldn't be the same without a big batch of them!

1 c. butter, softened
2 c. sugar
2 eggs, beaten
2 t. vanilla extract
1/2 c. buttermilk

4-1/2 to 6 c. all-purpose flour
2 t. baking powder
1 t. baking soda
1/2 t. salt

Blend together butter and sugar until smooth; add eggs and vanilla. Mix until very light. Add buttermilk and mix lightly. In a separate bowl, combine 4-1/2 cups flour, baking powder, baking soda and salt. Gradually add to butter mixture. Add more flour, just a little at a time, to make a soft dough that holds together. Wrap with plastic wrap; chill until firm, 2 hours or more. Divide dough in half; refrigerate one half and roll out remaining half, onto a lightly floured surface to 1/2-inch thick. Cut into desired shapes; transfer to ungreased baking sheets. Repeat with remaining dough. Bake at 350 degrees for 6 to 8 minutes, until lightly golden. Cool completely; frost. Makes 5 dozen.

Buttercream Frosting:

1 c. butter, softened
32-oz. pkg. powdered sugar
1 t. vanilla extract

1/4 to 1/2 c. milk
Optional: food coloring

Beat butter with powdered sugar until light. Add vanilla and 1/4 cup milk; beat until fluffy. Add more milk to reach desired consistency. Divide into smaller bowls; color each with a few drops of food coloring, if desired.

ℂlever **CUT-OUTS**

Scottish Jam Biscuits

Vickie

Mom always decorated these yummy cookie sandwiches with a candied red or green cherry half pressed into the frosting.

1/2 c. butter, softened	1 T. baking powder
1/2 c. sugar	1 T. allspice
2 eggs	1 T. cinnamon
2 c. all-purpose flour	1 c. strawberry jam

With an electric mixer on low speed, blend butter and sugar until smooth. Beat in eggs, one a time, mixing well after each addition. In a separate bowl, combine flour, baking powder and spices; stir into butter mixture to form a very stiff dough. Roll out on a lightly floured surface to 1/8 to 1/4-inch thick. Cut dough with a round cookie cutter. Place 2 inches apart onto ungreased baking sheets. Bake at 350 degrees for 10 minutes, or until edges start to turn golden. Cool completely on wire racks. Spread jam onto flat side of half the cookies; top with another cookie to make a sandwich. Spread frosting on top. Makes about 1-1/2 dozen.

Frosting:

1/2 c. butter, softened	1/4 c. milk, or as needed
1/8 t. salt	1-1/2 t. vanilla extract
3 c. powdered sugar	

Beat butter and salt together until soft. Gradually mix in powdered sugar, milk and vanilla until smooth and light.

Grandma Tremain's Nutmeg Cookies *Kathy Tremain*
Lawrenceburg, IN

My grandmother's nutmeg cookies bring back so many memories. My mother and I made them together every Christmas. We iced most of them, but my dad always insisted that some cookies be brushed with milk and sprinkled with sugar before they were baked. Now I use the same metal cookie cutters Mother and Grandmother used to use.

1 c. shortening
2 c. sugar
3 eggs, beaten
4 c. all-purpose flour
1 t. baking powder

1 t. baking soda
3 T. nutmeg
1/2 c. milk
2 T. white vinegar
Optional: frosting

Blend shortening and sugar together; add eggs. Slowly add flour, baking powder, baking soda and nutmeg. In a separate bowl, combine milk and vinegar; slowly stir into dough. Dough will be very sticky. Turn out onto a floured surface, one-half of dough at a time. Roll to 1/4-inch thick. Cut out with cookie cutters; place on parchment-paper lined baking sheets. Bake at 350 degrees for 10 minutes. Cool and frost as desired. Makes 3 dozen.

To stir up frosting in the reddest red, the greenest green and other extra bright holiday colors, choose paste-style food coloring...a little goes a long way! You'll find it at craft and cake decorating stores.

Clever CUT-OUTS

Santa's Spice Cookies

Sheri Dulaney
Englewood, OH

The little bit of spice in this recipe makes all the difference! No matter whether you sprinkle them with sugar before baking, or frost them after they're cooled, these cookies are scrumptious.

1 c. shortening
1 c. sugar
1 egg, beaten
1 t. vanilla extract
2 c. all-purpose flour

1/2 t. cream of tartar
1/2 t. baking soda
1/4 t. salt
1/4 t. nutmeg
1/4 t. ground ginger

Combine shortening, sugar, egg and vanilla until creamy; set aside. In a small bowl, mix together flour, cream of tartar, baking soda, salt, nutmeg and ginger. Gradually add to shortening mixture. Turn out onto a lightly floured surface. Roll out to 1/4-inch thick; cut out shapes with favorite cookie cutters. Transfer to baking sheets that have been sprayed with non-stick vegetable spray. Bake at 400 degrees for 6 to 8 minutes. Makes 2 to 3 dozen.

Handprint cookies...how sweet! Have kids place their hands on cookie dough and have a grown-up cut around carefully with a table knife. After baking, kids will love adding their names, "rings" and other details with frosting.

Grammie's Mincemeat Tartlets

Lisa Ludwig
Fort Wayne, IN

Christmas Eve at Grammie and Grampie's house was always the most anticipated day of the entire year! My younger sister and I were always filled with excitement and wonder. After the Christmas gifts were opened, Grammie always brought out all kinds of sweet treats, including these mincemeat-filled cookies. I wish we could go back to those precious times.

3/4 c. shortening	1/2 t. salt
1 c. sugar	1/3 c. milk
2 eggs, beaten	1/2 t. vanilla extract
3-1/2 c. all-purpose flour	29-oz. jar mincemeat
1 T. baking powder	Garnish: powdered sugar

Blend together shortening and sugar; add eggs. Combine flour, baking powder and salt; set aside. In small bowl, mix together milk and vanilla. Add to shortening mixture alternately with flour mixture. Chill dough. Roll out to 1/4-inch thick and cut with a round cookie or scalloped biscuit cutter. Place about one tablespoon mincemeat in the center of each; fold over and press edge with a wet fork to seal. Bake at 400 degrees for 10 to 15 minutes. Sprinkle lightly with powdered sugar while still warm. Makes about 2-1/2 dozen.

Start a tasty Advent tradition. Place 24 individually wrapped treats inside a cookie jar. Each day, beginning December 1st, little ones can reach in and enjoy a treat. When all the treats are gone, Santa's on his way!

Best-Ever
BAR COOKIES

Packing & Mailing Cookies

College students, service men and women, friends &
family...who wouldn't love to receive a care package
of homebaked cookies? Follow these simple steps to
ensure that cookies arrive fresh and whole.

○ ❄ ○

Select sturdy cookies that won't crumble easily. Bar
cookies, brownies and drop cookies are good travelers,
while frosted or filled cookies may be too soft.

○ ❄ ○

If you have your heart set on mailing sugar cookies, choose
cookie cutters without breakable details like fat snowmen,
round ornaments or simple Christmas trees. Decorate
with colored sugar or durable royal icing.

○ ❄ ○

Wrap cookies in pairs, back to back, with plastic wrap.
Double-wrap with aluminum foil to ensure freshness.

○ ❄ ○

Choose a sturdy box for mailing. Arrange wrapped cookies
in layers to fill the box...place them in a holiday tin first
if you like. Cushion layers with bubble wrap, plastic grocery
bags, crushed wax paper, packing peanuts or
even air-popped popcorn.

Turtle Pecan Bars

Janet Allen
Hauser, ID

These chocolatey caramel pecan bars will really go fast!

1 c. all-purpose flour
1/2 c. brown sugar, packed
1/2 c. butter
14-oz. can sweetened
   condensed milk
2 t. vanilla extract

2 c. chopped pecans
1 c. sweetened flaked coconut
20 vanilla caramels, unwrapped
2 T. milk
1 c. semi-sweet chocolate chips

Stir together flour and brown sugar. Cut in butter with a pastry blender until mixture resembles very coarse meal. Press mixture into an ungreased 13"x9" baking pan. Bake at 350 degrees for 15 minutes; remove from oven. Combine condensed milk and vanilla. Pour evenly over baked crust; sprinkle with pecans and coconut. Bake at 350 degrees for 25 to 30 minutes, until filling is set. Set pan on a wire rack to cool for 10 minutes. Combine caramels and milk in a small saucepan over medium-low heat. Cook and stir until caramels are melted; drizzle over top. Sprinkle with chocolate chips. Cool completely on a wire rack; cut into small bars. Makes 4 dozen.

Here's a trick to make perfect bar cookies. Lay a length of aluminum foil across the baking pan, extending a few inches on each side. Grease, fill and bake as directed. After cooling, use the extra foil as handles to lift out the cookies. Place on a cutting board and cut neatly into squares. So simple!

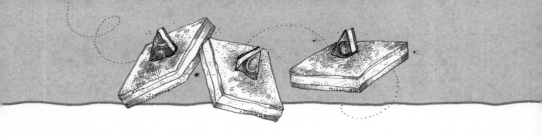

Toffee-Walnut Bars

Cindy Neel
Gooseberry Patch

A stack of these sweet bars on a doily-covered plate says,
"I'm glad you've come to visit!"

1 c. butter, softened
1/2 c. brown sugar, packed
1/2 t. salt
3 T. milk
1 t. vanilla extract

1-1/2 c. all-purpose flour
1 c. chopped walnuts, divided
6 1.55-oz. milk chocolate
     candy bars

Beat butter with an electric mixer on medium-high speed for
30 seconds. Add brown sugar and salt; blend until combined. Add
milk and vanilla; stir in as much flour as possible with mixer. Stir in
remaining flour with a wooden spoon; stir in half the nuts. Spread
batter in a greased 13"x9" baking pan. Bake at 350 degrees for
20 to 25 minutes, until lightly golden around edges. Arrange
chocolate bars on top of hot crust. Let stand for a few minutes, until
chocolate is melted. Spread chocolate evenly over crust. Sprinkle with
remaining nuts. Cool in pan on a wire rack; slice into bars. Makes
3 dozen.

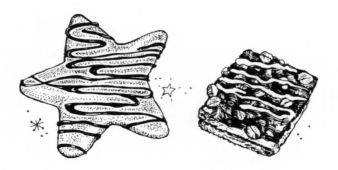

For dazzling bar cookies, melt 1/2 cup chocolate chips with a teaspoon
of shortening. Drizzle over uncut bars. Sprinkle with chopped nuts,
sugar crystals or crushed candy canes for an extra-special finish.
No one will believe they didn't come from a bakery!

Frosted Mocha Brownies

Connie Bryant
Topeka, KS

You'll never go back to brownies from a mix after you've tasted these yummy chocolate-frosted brownies.

1 c. sugar
1/2 c. plus 3 T. butter, softened
  and divided
1/3 c. plus 1/4 c. baking cocoa,
  divided
1 t. instant coffee granules
2 eggs, beaten
1-1/2 t. vanilla extract, divided
2/3 c. all-purpose flour
1/2 t. baking powder
1/4 t. salt
1/2 c. chopped walnuts
2 c. powdered sugar, divided
2 to 3 T. milk

Combine sugar, 1/2 cup butter, 1/3 cup baking cocoa and coffee granules in a medium saucepan. Cook and stir over medium heat until butter is melted. Remove from heat; cool for 5 minutes. Add eggs and one teaspoon vanilla; mix just until combined. Stir in flour, baking powder and salt; add nuts. Spread batter in a greased 9"x9" baking pan. Bake at 350 degrees for 25 minutes, or until set. Cool in pan on a wire rack. Beat remaining butter until light and fluffy; add remaining cocoa. Gradually add one cup powdered sugar, mixing well. Stir in 2 tablespoons milk and remaining vanilla. Gradually stir in remaining powdered sugar and additional milk as needed to make a spreading consistency. Spread over cooled brownies; slice into bars. Makes one dozen.

A gift for the person who has everything...a retro tin lunchbox featuring his or her favorite childhood cartoon character! Fill it with homemade cookies and old-fashioned candies... they'll feel like a kid again.

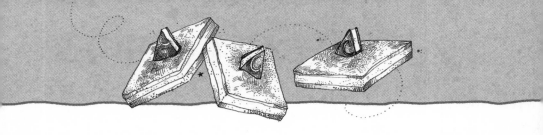

Classic Lemon Bars

Karen Streitberger
West Jordan, UT

Cut into bite-size squares and place in ruffled paper mini muffin liners to set a pretty tea table.

1 c. butter, softened
2-1/4 c. all-purpose flour,
   divided
1/2 c. powdered sugar
1/8 t. salt

2 c. sugar
4 eggs, beaten
6 T. lemon juice
Garnish: additional powdered
   sugar

Combine butter, 2 cups flour, powdered sugar and salt; mix well. Press into an ungreased 13"x9" baking pan. Bake at 350 degrees for 15 minutes until golden. Combine sugar and remaining flour in a large bowl; stir in eggs and lemon juice. Pour onto slightly cooled crust. Bake at 350 degrees for 25 minutes. Cool; sprinkle with powdered sugar. Slice into bars. Makes 15 to 18.

Dress up frosted bar cookies in a snap. Set a cookie cutter on top and use a teaspoon to sprinkle colored sugar inside. Carefully lift off the cutter...done!

Cranberry Crumb Bars

Jo Ann

*We can't wait 'til Christmas for these sweet-tart bar cookies...
they've become a tradition for our family's
Thanksgiving dinner too.*

1-1/2 c. plus 1/3 c. all-purpose
  flour, divided
1/3 c. powdered sugar
1 c. butter, chilled and divided
8-oz. pkg. cream cheese,
  softened
14-oz. can sweetened
  condensed milk

1/4 c. lemon juice
2 T. cornstarch
3 T. brown sugar, packed and
  divided
16-oz. can whole-berry
  cranberry sauce
3/4 c. walnuts, finely chopped

Combine 1-1/2 cups flour and powdered sugar; cut in 3/4 cup
butter until crumbly. Press into a greased 13"x9" baking pan. Bake at
350 degrees for 15 to 20 minutes, until edges are golden. Remove
from oven. Beat cream cheese until smooth. Add condensed milk and
lemon juice; mix well and spread over baked crust. In a separate bowl,
combine cornstarch and one tablespoon brown sugar. Stir in cranberry
sauce until combined. Spread over cream cheese layer and set aside.
Combine brown sugar and remaining flour; cut in remaining butter.
Stir in nuts; sprinkle over filling. Bake at 325 degrees for 40 to
45 minutes, until topping is golden. Cool in pan on a wire rack.
Cover and chill for 3 hours before slicing into bars. Makes one dozen.

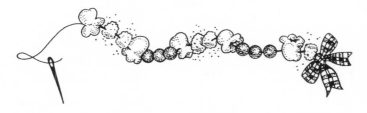

Spend a cozy evening in front of the fireplace, stringing popcorn and
fresh cranberries to wind around the Christmas tree. Be sure to have
some cookies to enjoy and hot cider to sip...memories in the making!

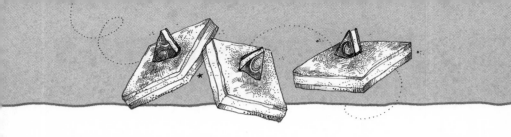

Scotch Oatmeal Bars

Alice Stone
Shalimar, FL

An easy one-bowl recipe.

3/4 c. butter, softened
3 c. long-cooking oats,
   uncooked
2/3 c. sugar
1/2 c. all-purpose flour

2/3 c. semi-sweet chocolate
   chunks
1 t. vanilla extract
1/2 t. salt

Stir together all ingredients by hand until well blended. Press into an ungreased 13"x9" baking pan. Bake at 350 degrees for 30 minutes. Cut into bars. Makes 1-1/2 dozen.

Make a holiday memory tray! Paint a wooden tray with craft paint. When dry, arrange cut-outs from favorite photos and Christmas cards on the tray. Glue them in place using découpage medium, then brush another layer or two over top and sprinkle with glitter.

Best-Ever **BAR COOKIES**

Grammy's Tom Thumb Bars

Bonnie Studler
Los Angeles, CA

Grammy always had homemade treats for my sister and me. These tiny bars are chewy, moist and deliciously sweet...we hope you enjoy them!

1/2 c. shortening
1-1/2 c. dark brown sugar,
   packed and divided
1/2 t. salt
1 c. plus 2 T. all-purpose flour
1/2 t. baking powder

2 eggs, beaten
1 t. vanilla extract
1-1/2 c. sweetened flaked
   coconut
1 c. chopped walnuts

Combine shortening and 1/2 cup brown sugar until smooth. Stir in salt and one cup flour until well blended. Press into a greased 13"x9" baking pan. Bake at 325 degrees for 15 minutes, or until golden. Remove from oven; let cool. In a separate bowl, mix together remaining brown sugar, baking powder and remaining flour until well blended. Mix in eggs and vanilla, beating until thick and foamy. Stir in coconut and nuts; spread over baked crust. Bake at 350 degrees for 35 minutes, or until bars are lightly golden and puffy. Cool completely; slice into 36 tiny bars. Makes 3 dozen.

For the best bar cookies, be sure to use the pan size that the recipe calls for...otherwise, the baking time may be affected.

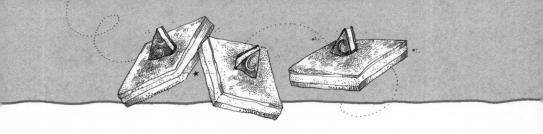

Butterscotch Cheesecake Bars

Marsha Konken
Sterling, CO

A bake sale favorite.

6-oz. pkg. butterscotch chips
1/3 c. butter
2 c. graham cracker crumbs
1 c. chopped pecans
8-oz. pkg. cream cheese,
   softened

14-oz. can sweetened
   condensed milk
1 t. vanilla extract
1 egg, beaten

Melt butterscotch chips and butter in a saucepan over medium-low heat; stir in cracker crumbs and pecans. Press half of mixture into an ungreased 13"x9" baking pan. Beat cream cheese in a large bowl until fluffy; stir in condensed milk. Add vanilla and egg; mix well and pour over crumb mixture. Top with remaining crumb mixture. Bake at 350 degrees for 25 to 30 minutes. Chill until firm; cut into bars. Makes about 1-1/2 dozen.

Brighten up a party coffee tray...stir a teaspoon of sparkly
red decorator sugar into the sugar bowl!

Best-Ever **BAR COOKIES**

Carol's Sopaipilla Bars

Carol Hickman
Kingsport, TN

*These cream-filled bars are delicious any time of day,
even with a cup of tea or coffee at breakfast.*

2 8-oz. tubes refrigerated
   crescent rolls, divided
8-oz. pkg. cream cheese,
   softened
1-1/2 c. sugar, divided

1 t. vanilla extract
1 t. cinnamon
1/2 c. butter, melted

Press one tube crescent rolls into an ungreased 13"x9" baking pan; set aside. Combine cream cheese, one cup sugar and vanilla in a small bowl. Spread cream cheese mixture over crescents in baking pan. Arrange remaining crescent rolls over cream cheese layer. In a small bowl, combine remaining sugar and cinnamon; sprinkle over crescents. Drizzle melted butter over top. Bake at 350 degrees for 25 to 30 minutes. Cool to room temperature; slice into bars. Makes about 1-1/2 dozen.

Don't overlook unusual sources for clever cookie containers!
Craft stores have holiday-print fabric for making gift bags plus
lots of ribbons and trims. Office supply stores have mailing tubes
plus stickers & seals...there are even shiny new aluminum
paint cans and paper paint pails at the hardware store.

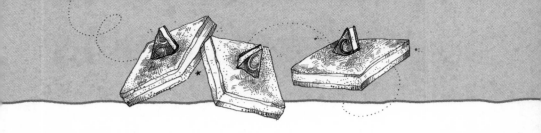

Trail Bars

Meri Hebert
Cheboygan, MI

*After delivering gifts all night long, Santa would love to find a
plate of these tasty, healthy treats left by the Christmas tree!*

1 c. creamy peanut butter
1 c. honey
1 c. semi-sweet chocolate chips

4 c. quick-cooking oats,
uncooked

Mix together peanut butter and honey; stir in chocolate chips and
oats. Press into a lightly greased 13"x9" baking pan. Cover and
refrigerate until ready to serve; cut into bars. Makes 1-1/2 dozen.

A great gift for a nature enthusiast! Wrap several Trail Bars
in plastic wrap to give with a guidebook to hiking
trails, wild birds or rock collecting.

Best-Ever **BAR COOKIES**

Choco-Berry Goodie Bars

Brenda Smith
Gooseberry Patch

These bars are packed with yummy stuff! It's easy to change them to suit your family's taste too...try using chopped walnuts or pecans instead of almonds and chopped dried apricots or pineapple instead of cranberries.

3 c. quick-cooking oats, uncooked
14-oz. can sweetened condensed milk
2 T. butter, melted
1 c. sweetened flaked coconut

1 c. sliced almonds
1 c. mini semi-sweet chocolate chips
1/2 c. sweetened dried cranberries

Combine all ingredients in a large bowl; use hands to mix well. Press into a greased 13"x9" baking pan. Bake at 350 degrees for 20 to 25 minutes, until edges are golden. Cool for 5 minutes; slice into squares and cool completely. Makes 2 dozen.

Have a cookies & punch party! Bake and freeze cookies in advance, as time allows. The day before, mix up a punch to refrigerate and remove cookies from the freezer. At party time, just pour punch into a punch bowl, arrange cookies on trays and greet your guests.

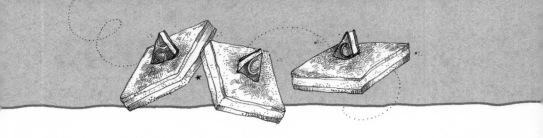

Cashew-Macadamia Crunch

Marilyn Miller
Fort Washington, PA

*If you've been very, very good this year, maybe Santa will
bring you some of this fabulous chocolate candy!*

12-oz. pkg. milk chocolate chips
1/2 c. butter, softened
1/2 c. sugar
2 T. light corn syrup

3/4 c. cashews, coarsely
   chopped
3/4 c. macadamia nuts, coarsely
   chopped

Line a 9"x9" baking pan with aluminum foil extending over edges of
pan. Sprinkle chocolate chips in pan; set aside. Combine butter, sugar,
corn syrup and nuts in a skillet over low heat, stirring constantly.
Cook until butter is melted and sugar is dissolved. Increase heat to
medium, stirring constantly; cook until mixture begins to cling together and turns golden. Pour over chocolate chips in pan, spreading
evenly. Cool; refrigerate until firm. Remove from pan using aluminum
foil edges as a handle; peel off foil. Break into pieces. Makes about
2 pounds.

White Hot Chocolate

Geneva Rogers
Gillette, WY

Use whole milk for the richest flavor.

6-oz. pkg. white chocolate chips
1/2 to 1 t. cinnamon
Optional: 1/4 t. cayenne pepper

1 egg, beaten
3-1/4 c. milk, divided
Optional: additional cinnamon

Place chocolate chips in a metal bowl over a pan of barely simmering water. Stir until smooth. Stir in spices; whisk in egg until smooth.
Gradually whisk in one cup milk until blended, about 2 minutes. Stir
in remaining milk; heat until hot but not boiling. Ladle into mugs;
sprinkle with additional cinnamon, if desired. Serves 4.

Old-Fashioned Toffee

Michelle Filz
Union Grove, WI

Wrapped in a decorative container, this is a
great hostess gift for the holidays.

1 c. butter
1-1/3 c. sugar
1/8 t. salt

1 T. light corn syrup
3 T. water
12-oz. pkg. milk chocolate chips

Melt butter in a large saucepan over medium heat. Add sugar, salt, corn syrup and water. Cook, stirring occasionally, until a candy thermometer reaches 275 degrees. Continue to cook, stirring constantly, until candy thermometer reaches 300 degrees. Spread onto an ungreased baking sheet; cool completely. Melt half of chocolate chips; spread over cooled toffee. Cool completely. Cover with another baking sheet and turn over. Melt remaining chocolate chips and spread over other side. Cool completely. Break into one to 2-inch pieces. Makes about 2 pounds.

Colorful vintage holiday cookie tins can be found at tag sales...
just pop in a parchment paper lining and they're ready to fill
with baked goodies for gift giving.

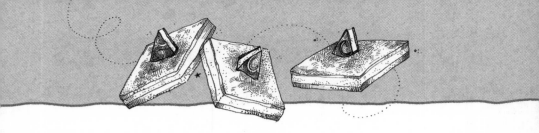

Sharon's Gumdrop Bars

Sharon Crider
Junction City, KS

These bars with their jewel-like pieces of gumdrops are very tasty.
I used to bake them for my children as they were growing up...
they're still a favorite of mine.

1/2 c. butter
1/2 t. baking powder
1-1/2 c. brown sugar, packed
1/2 t. salt
2 eggs, beaten

1/2 c. chopped nuts
1-1/2 c. all-purpose flour
1 c. gumdrops, chopped
1 t. vanilla extract
Garnish: powdered sugar

Melt butter in a saucepan; stir in remaining ingredients except powdered sugar. Spread in a greased and floured 13"x9" baking pan. Bake at 350 degrees for 25 to 30 minutes, until golden. Sprinkle with powdered sugar. Cool and slice into bars. Makes 2 dozen.

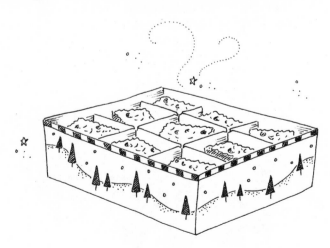

Sharon's Gumdrop Bars can be slipped inside a vintage Christmas ornament box for gift giving. Just line the box with wax paper, then store in the freezer until it's time for the annual cookie exchange or visit to a neighbor's home.

Sugarplum Cookie Pizza

Audrey Lett
Newark, DE

*Such a fun dessert to serve! Sprinkle cashew halves
and dark chocolate chips over the white chocolate
drizzle for a really decadent treat.*

2/3 c. butter, softened
3/4 c. sugar
1/2 t. baking soda
1 t. ground ginger
1/2 t. cinnamon
1 egg, beaten

2 T. molasses
1-3/4 c. all-purpose flour
1-3/4 c. mini gumdrops
1/2 c. white chocolate chips
1-1/2 t. butter-flavored
   shortening

In a large bowl, with an electric mixer on medium-high speed, beat
butter for 30 seconds. Add sugar, baking soda and spices; beat until
combined. Beat in egg and molasses; beat in as much flour as possible
with mixer. Use a wooden spoon to stir in any remaining flour.
Pat evenly into a lightly greased 12" round pizza pan. Bake at
350 degrees for 12 minutes. Sprinkle gumdrops over baked crust;
bake an additional 8 minutes, or until edges are golden. Cool
completely in pan on a wire rack. In a small saucepan over low heat,
melt chocolate chips and shortening; drizzle over cookie. Let stand
20 to 30 minutes, until set; cut into thin wedges. Makes 16 servings.

A pizza cutter is handy for cutting brownies and bar cookies neatly.
Dip the cutter into warm water between cuts.

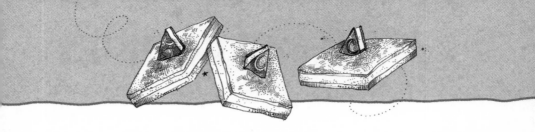

Teresa's Tasty Apricot Bars

Teresa Stiegelmeyer
Indianapolis, IN

*This yummy bar cookie packs well for a pitch-in dinner.
Sometimes I like to substitute raspberry preserves
for a whole new taste.*

1 c. all-purpose flour
1 t. baking powder
1/2 c. margarine, softened

1 egg, beaten
1 T. milk
3/4 c. apricot preserves

Combine flour, baking powder and margarine; add egg and milk. Press into a greased 9"x9" baking pan; spread with preserves and set aside. Spread Coconut Topping over preserves. Bake at 350 degrees for 25 to 30 minutes. Cut into bars. Makes one dozen.

Coconut Topping:

1/4 c. margarine, softened
1 c. sugar
1 egg, beaten

1 t. vanilla extract
1 c. sweetened flaked coconut

Combine margarine and sugar. Add egg and vanilla; stir in coconut.

May peace be your gift at CHRISTMAS & Your Blessing all year through. —author unknown

Fruity Popcorn Bars

Melody Taynor
Everett, WA

A perfect pick-me-up on a busy shopping day.

3-oz. pkg. microwave popcorn, popped
3/4 c. white chocolate chips
3/4 c. sweetened dried cranberries
1/2 c. sweetened flaked coconut
1/2 c. slivered almonds, coarsely chopped
10-oz. pkg. marshmallows
3 T. butter

Line a 13"x9" baking pan with aluminum foil; spray lightly with non-stick vegetable spray. Toss together popcorn, chocolate chips, cranberries, coconut and almonds in a large bowl; set aside. Melt marshmallows and butter in a saucepan over medium heat; stir until smooth. Pour over popcorn mixture and toss to coat completely; quickly pour into prepared pan. Lay a sheet of wax paper over top and press down firmly. Chill for 30 minutes, or until firm. Lift bars from pan, using foil as handles; peel off foil and wax paper. Slice into bars and chill an additional 30 minutes. Makes 16.

Spoon the dry ingredients for Fruity Popcorn Bars into separate plastic zipping bags and nestle in a cheery red mixing bowl along with the packages of popcorn and marshmallows. Tie on a recipe card for a gift anyone is sure to love!

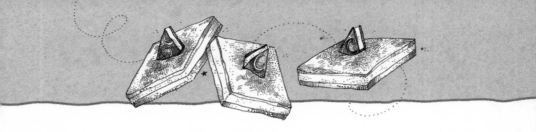

Grandma Fry's Nanaimo Bars

Stella Jensen
Cape Girardeau, MO

*A Canadian treat. My mother always made these for special
occasions when I was growing up, and now I make
them to remember her by.*

1 c. plus 1 T. butter, softened
and divided
1/4 c. sugar
1-oz. sq. unsweetened baking
chocolate, chopped
1 t. vanilla extract
1 egg, beaten
2 c. graham cracker crumbs

1/2 c. chopped nuts
1 c. sweetened flaked coconut
2 T. instant vanilla pudding mix
2 c. powdered sugar
3 T. milk
4 1-oz. sqs. semi-sweet baking
chocolate, chopped

Combine 1/2 cup butter, sugar and unsweetened chocolate in a double
boiler over medium heat. Cook until well blended; stir in vanilla. Add
egg; cook for 5 minutes. Remove from heat; stir in crumbs, nuts and
coconut. Press into a greased 13"x9" baking pan; chill for 15 minutes.
Beat 1/2 cup butter until fluffy; stir in pudding mix, powdered sugar
and milk. Spread over mixture. Melt semi-sweet chocolate and
remaining butter over low heat until well blended. Spread over top;
chill before cutting into bars. Makes about 3-1/2 dozen.

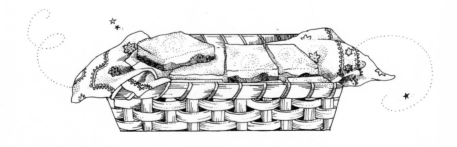

Deliver a tray of cookies and fresh fruit or homemade bread to a
nursing home, an elderly neighbor or a friend who needs cheering.

Chocolate Chip Shortbread

Nancy Girard
Chesapeake, VA

This recipe has become a standard for our Christmas cookie plate. It is one of our favorites...light and buttery with that irresistible taste of chocolate!

1 c. butter, softened
1/3 c. sugar
1-3/4 c. all-purpose flour

1/4 c. cornstarch
1 c. mini semi-sweet chocolate
   chips

Combine butter and sugar in a large bowl. With an electric mixer, beat at medium speed until creamy, one to 2 minutes. Reduce speed to low. Add flour and cornstarch; beat until well mixed, one to 2 minutes. Stir in chips. Press into an ungreased 13"x9" baking pan; pierce all over with a fork. Bake at 350 degrees for 35 to 45 minutes, just until edges begin to turn golden. If edges begin getting too dark, cover with aluminum foil. Cool in pan 15 minutes; slice into bars while still warm. Makes 1-1/2 dozen.

After Christmas dinner, a simple dessert is perfect.
Enjoy assorted Christmas cookies accompanied
by scoops of pink peppermint ice cream.

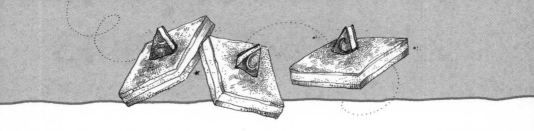

Ooey-Gooey S'mores Squares

Denise Bushnell
Centreville, VA

My sister and I first tried this recipe while enjoying a wonderful vacation at our beloved Lake George, where s'mores are a staple.

2 sleeves graham crackers, crushed and divided
1/4 c. sugar, divided
1 c. butter, melted and divided
8 1.55-oz. milk chocolate candy bars, divided

7-oz. jar marshmallow creme, divided
1 sleeve chocolate graham crackers, crushed

Combine plain graham cracker crumbs and sugar; stir in 2/3 cup butter. Set aside half of crumb mixture; press the rest into a lightly greased 8"x8" baking pan. Bake at 325 degrees for 10 minutes; cool slightly. Break chocolate bars in half; spread with marshmallow creme. Arrange half the bars over crust, breaking into smaller pieces to make them fit. Combine chocolate graham cracker crumbs with remaining butter. Spread mixture over marshmallow creme-covered chocolate bars; press gently. Arrange remaining chocolate bars over chocolate graham layer. Spread reserved plain crumb mixture over top; press down gently. Bake at 325 degrees for 15 to 20 minutes. Cool completely, about 90 minutes to 2 hours. Slice into squares. Makes 16 to 25.

S'mores, campfires and ghost stories are a classic combination. Why not whip up a batch of Ooey-Gooey S'mores Squares to snack on and gather the family by the fireplace for a reading of *A Christmas Carol*?

Peanut Butter Bars

Kristin Pittis
Dennison, OH

*These bars were always everyone's favorite treat in our school cafeteria.
When I went back to school as a substitute teacher, they were still
serving these bars...they were every bit as delicious as I remembered.
I begged Pat, the head cook, for the recipe and she kindly obliged.
Thanks, Pat!*

1/2 c. butter, softened
1/2 c. sugar
1/2 c. brown sugar, packed
1 egg, beaten
1/2 c. creamy peanut butter
1/2 t. baking soda

1/4 t. salt
1/2 t. vanilla extract
1 c. all-purpose flour
1 c. long-cooking oats,
    uncooked

Combine butter and sugars in a large bowl. Add egg, peanut butter,
baking soda, salt and vanilla; stir in flour and oats. Spread into
a greased 13"x9" baking pan. Bake at 350 degrees for 20 to
25 minutes; cool and frost with Peanut Butter Icing. Cut into bars.
Makes 2 dozen.

Peanut Butter Icing:

1/2 c. butter, softened
1 c. creamy peanut butter

2 c. powdered sugar
3 T. milk

Beat butter and peanut butter together until smooth. Gradually add
powdered sugar. Beat in milk, one tablespoon at a time, as mixture
gets thicker. Beat for 3 minutes, until fluffy.

Just for fun...tie up a gift
package using brightly
colored novelty shoestrings
instead of ribbon.

Irene's Molasses Squares

Irene Nelson
Dexter, ME

*Chopped walnuts, dates or raisins make a nice addition
to this old-fashioned recipe.*

1/2 c. molasses
1/2 c. shortening
1/2 c. brown sugar, packed
1 egg, beaten
1/2 c. milk
2 t. vanilla extract, divided

2 c. all-purpose flour
1-1/2 t. baking powder
1/4 t. baking soda
1/2 t. salt
1 c. powdered sugar
2 to 3 T. milk

Combine first 6 ingredients in a large bowl; mix well. Blend together flour, baking powder, baking soda and salt; gradually add to molasses mixture. Spread into a greased 13"x9" baking pan. Bake at 350 degrees for 20 minutes. Combine powdered sugar, remaining vanilla and milk; mix well. Spread over top while warm. Slice into squares. Makes 2 dozen.

A friend who bakes would love to find a cookbook slipped in the pocket of a potholder. Don't forget to tuck in recipe cards sharing some family favorites too.

Date & Walnut Bars

Lee Ann Ritchotte
Manchester, NH

My favorite! The filling is so full of dates, just the way I like it.
As far back as I can remember, my grandmother and
mother always made them.

16-oz. pkg. chopped dates
3/4 c. sugar
1 c. water
1 t. vanilla extract
1 c. chopped walnuts
3/4 c. plus 1 T. butter, melted
   and divided

1-3/4 c. long-cooking oats,
   uncooked
1-1/2 c. all-purpose flour
1/2 t. baking powder
1 t. baking soda
1/2 t. salt
1 c. brown sugar, packed

Combine dates, sugar and water in a large saucepan over medium heat. Bring to a boil; simmer for 5 to 10 minutes, until thick. Stir in vanilla, walnuts and one tablespoon butter; set aside to cool slightly. Combine remaining ingredients, including butter. Press half of oat mixture into a lightly greased 13"x9" baking pan; spread date mixture over top. Cover with remaining half of oat mixture; press lightly. Bake at 350 degrees for 25 minutes. Cool completely before slicing into squares. Makes 2 to 2-1/2 dozen.

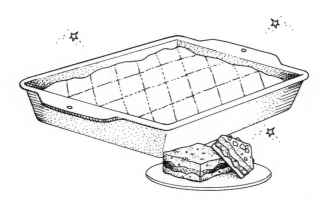

Cut square bar cookies diagonally to form
triangles for a whole new look.

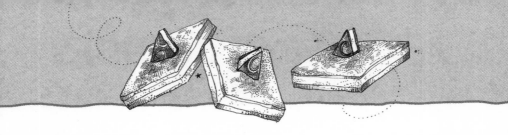

Raspberry-Lemon Bars

Rhonda Reeder
Ellicott City, MD

Mom has a real sweet tooth, but wanted to cut back on calories. She was so happy when I first served her these tart, lemony bars...you'd never guess this is a "light" recipe!

3/4 c. plus 2 T. all-purpose flour, divided
2 c. powdered calorie-free sweetener, divided
1/8 t. salt
1/4 c. butter

1/2 c. egg substitute
1/2 c. half-and-half
1/2 c. lemon juice
1 T. lemon zest
1/4 c. reduced-sugar raspberry preserves

Mix together 3/4 cup flour, 3/4 cup sweetener and salt in a medium bowl. Cut in butter until mixture is crumbly. Press dough into a lightly greased 8"x8" baking pan. Bake at 350 degrees for 15 to 20 minutes, until golden. Combine remaining sweetener and flour in a medium bowl; mix well. Add egg substitute and half-and-half; stir until blended. Slowly add lemon juice, stirring constantly; stir in zest. Spread preserves evenly over warm crust. Gently pour lemon mixture over preserves. Bake at 350 degrees for 20 to 25 minutes, until set. Remove from oven; cool completely. Chill for 2 hours before cutting into bars. Makes 16 to 20.

Freshly grated citrus zest adds so much flavor to recipes, and it's easy to keep on hand. Whenever you use an orange, lemon or lime, just grate the peel first. Keep it frozen in an airtight container for up to 2 months.

Ashley's Apple Butter Bars

Debbie White
Williamson, WV

This is one of the first recipes my daughter, Ashley, tried when she started baking as a little girl. She's married now and this recipe still remains a family favorite.

1-1/2 c. all-purpose flour
1 t. baking soda
1 t. salt
1-1/2 c. quick-cooking oats, uncooked

1-1/2 c. sugar
1 c. butter, melted
1-1/2 c. apple butter
1 c. chopped pecans or walnuts

Combine flour, baking soda and salt in a large bowl. Stir in oats and sugar. Add melted butter; mix well until crumbly. Press half of mixture into a greased 13"x9" baking pan; set aside. Mix apple butter and nuts together; spread over crumb mixture. Sprinkle with remaining crumb mixture. Bake at 350 degrees for 50 to 60 minutes, until golden. Cool completely; slice into bars. Makes about 2-1/2 dozen.

Cut a pan of bar cookies into circles using a round cookie cutter.
Arrange cookies in a glass tumbler, separated by circles of wax paper.
Tie a circle of fabric with jute over the tumbler's top...clever!

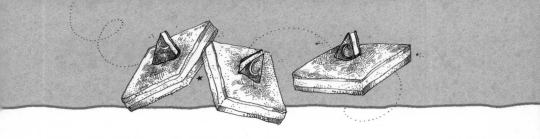

Brown Sugar Brownies

Melissa Hull
Pulaski, NY

*I found this recipe in my mom's recipe box. My daughters and
I tried it many times before we perfected it...my co-workers
were happy to serve as taste testers!*

2/3 c. butter, softened
2-1/4 c. brown sugar, packed
4 eggs, beaten
2 c. all-purpose flour
2 t. baking powder

1 t. salt
1 t. vanilla extract
6-oz. pkg. semi-sweet chocolate
　chips

With an electric mixer, beat together butter and brown sugar in a
small bowl; beat in eggs. In a separate bowl, mix together flour,
baking powder, salt and vanilla; mix in butter mixture. Stir in
chocolate chips; spoon batter into a greased 13"x9" baking pan.
Bake at 350 degrees for 35 to 40 minutes, until a toothpick tests
clean. Cut into squares. Makes about 1-1/2 dozen.

Crushed candy canes make a festive topping for frosted brownies.
Simply place in a plastic zipping bag and tap gently with a kitchen
mallet or even a cast-iron skillet until candy is broken up.

Orangey Brownies

Jackie Smulski
Lyons, IL

What a wonderful summery treat in the middle of winter!
The first bite will take you away to a Florida orange grove.

1-1/2 c. all-purpose flour
1-3/4 c. sugar
3/4 t. salt
1 c. butter, softened
4 eggs, beaten

2 t. orange extract
2 T. orange zest, divided
1 c. powdered sugar
2 T. orange juice

Stir together flour, sugar and salt in a large bowl; add butter, eggs, extract and one tablespoon zest. Beat mixture until well blended; pour into a greased 13"x9" baking pan. Bake at 350 degrees for 30 minutes, or until lightly golden and center is set. Remove from oven; pierce entire top with a fork. In a small bowl, mix together powdered sugar, orange juice and remaining zest; spread over brownies. Cool completely; slice into squares. Makes one dozen.

Flea-market finds like vintage pie plates, jelly jars and enamelware pails are sure to bring a smile when filled with holiday sweets!

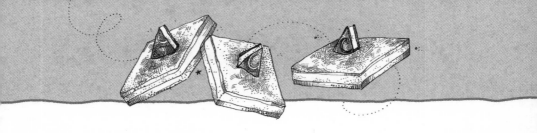

Caramel Oat Bars

Tori Willis
Champaign, IL

My kids like to help unwrap the caramel candies...
but I've found out the hard way that I'd better
have a few extras on hand for nibbling!

32 caramels, unwrapped
5 T. whipping cream
1 c. long-cooking oats,
   uncooked
1 c. all-purpose flour
3/4 c. brown sugar, packed

1/2 t. baking soda
1/4 t. salt
3/4 c. butter, melted
1/2 c. semi-sweet chocolate
   chips
1/2 c. chopped walnuts

Combine caramels and cream in a saucepan over low heat, stirring occasionally until smooth; set aside. Mix together oats, flour, brown sugar, baking soda and salt in a medium bowl; stir in melted butter until crumbly. Press half the mixture into a lightly greased 13"x9" baking pan. Bake at 350 degrees for 8 minutes. Remove from oven; sprinkle with chocolate chips and walnuts. Pour caramel mixture over top; sprinkle with remaining oat mixture. Return to oven and bake for an additional 12 minutes, or until top is lightly toasted. Slice into bars while still warm. Makes about 2 dozen.

When you go out on Christmas Eve to attend church or see the Christmas lights, why not drop off a dozen fresh-baked cookies at your local fire or police station?

Rocky Road Crunch Bars

Angie Biggin
Lyons, IL

Stir in some red & green chocolate-coated candies
for a holiday touch.

1/3 c. honey	2 T. creamy or crunchy peanut
3 T. butter	butter
4 c. mini marshmallows	4 1-oz. sqs. semi-sweet baking
4 c. granola or oat cluster cereal	chocolate, chopped

Combine honey and butter in a microwave-safe bowl; microwave on high setting for one minute. Stir until well blended. Add mini marshmallows; toss to coat. Microwave on high setting for 90 seconds, or until marshmallows are puffed. Stir in remaining ingredients. Press into a greased 13"x9" baking pan; chill. Cut into bars. Makes 2 dozen.

Once in a young lifetime, one should be allowed to have as much

sweetness as one can possibly want and hold.

-Judith Olney

107

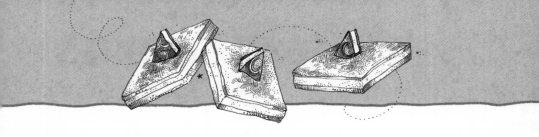

Chocolate Cherry Bars

Edith Bolstad
Beaver Dam, WI

Irresistible...and you won't believe how easy they are!

1/2 c. butter, melted
1-1/2 c. graham cracker crumbs
14-oz. can sweetened
    condensed milk

12-oz. pkg. milk chocolate chips
10-oz. jar maraschino cherries,
    drained and chopped

Spread melted butter evenly in a 13"x9" baking pan. Stir in graham cracker crumbs; press down to form a crust. Pour condensed milk over top; sprinkle with chocolate chips and chopped cherries. Bake at 350 degrees for 25 minutes. Cool completely; slice into bars. Makes about 2 dozen.

Wrap up some cookies in a sweet holiday apron...
don't forget to tuck the recipe in the pocket!

Brownie Mallow Bars

Nancy Johnson
Laverne, OK

One time I left out the cereal, and they still tasted delicious!

21-oz. pkg. fudge brownie mix
7-oz. jar marshmallow creme
12-oz. pkg. semi-sweet
   chocolate chips

1 c. creamy peanut butter
1 T. butter
1 c. crispy rice cereal

Prepare brownie mix according to package directions; pour into a greased 13"x9" baking pan. Bake at 350 degrees for 28 to 30 minutes. Carefully spread marshmallow creme over hot brownies; cool. Combine chocolate chips, peanut butter and butter in a microwave-safe bowl. Microwave on high setting for 2 to 3 minutes, stirring every 30 seconds, until smooth. Stir in cereal; mix gently and spread over brownies. Refrigerate for one to 2 hours until firm, before slicing into bars. Makes 2 to 2-1/2 dozen.

You'll find all kinds of paper tags, stickers, glitter and trims in the scrapbooking aisle of a nearby craft store...just right for creating handmade gift tags. Let your imagination go!

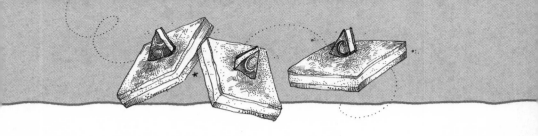

Apricot Nut Bars

Joan White
Malvern, PA

A crisp crust topped with sweet apricot preserves
and crunchy almonds...delectable!

1-1/2 c. all-purpose flour	1 egg, beaten
3/4 c. powdered sugar	1/2 c. sugar
1/2 c. plus 1 T. butter, softened	1/2 c. apricot preserves
and divided	1/2 t. vanilla extract
1/4 c. shortening	1 c. sliced almonds

Combine flour, powdered sugar, 1/2 cup butter and shortening
in a large bowl; beat until well blended. Pat into an ungreased
13"x9" baking pan. Bake at 350 degrees for 18 to 20 minutes, until
golden. In a small bowl, beat egg, sugar, preserves, remaining butter
and vanilla until smooth. Spread over hot crust; sprinkle with
almonds. Bake at 350 for 15 to 20 minutes. Cool and cut into bars.
Makes 2-1/2 to 3 dozen.

A sweet keepsake for a family brunch. Copy one of Grandma's
tried & true recipes onto a festive card, then punch a hole in the
corner and tie the card to a rolled napkin with a length of ribbon.

Scandinavian Almond Bars

Jennifer Wilken
Bourbonnais, IL

This recipe is one of my favorites that I make at Christmastime. It is light and very tasty, not a heavy dessert. These bars go wonderfully with a cup of coffee or hot tea...the perfect ending to a holiday meal.

1/2 c. butter, softened
1 c. sugar
1 egg, beaten
3/4 t. almond extract, divided
1-3/4 c. all-purpose flour

2 t. baking powder
1/4 t. salt
2 to 3 T. milk, divided
1/2 c. sliced almonds, chopped
1 c. powdered sugar

Blend together butter and sugar in a large bowl; beat in egg and 1/2 teaspoon extract. Combine flour, baking powder and salt; gradually add to butter mixture and mix well. Divide dough into fourths; form into 12"x3" rectangles. Place 5 inches apart on greased baking sheets. Brush with one tablespoon milk; sprinkle with almonds. Bake at 325 degrees for 18 to 20 minutes, until set and edges are golden. Cool on baking sheets for 5 minutes; cut diagonally into one-inch slices. Remove to wire racks to cool completely. Combine powdered sugar, remaining extract and enough of remaining milk to make a drizzling consistency; drizzle over bars. Makes 4 dozen.

Wrap up homebaked cookies in a jiffy! Stamp a gift bag with rubber stamps and add a tag to match... pop in a plastic zipping bag of cookies and they're ready to give!

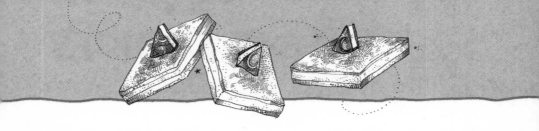

Pumpkin Jingle Bars

JoAnna Nicoline-Haughey
Berwyn, PA

*Short on time? Just sprinkle these tasty bars with
powdered sugar instead of frosting and decorating.*

18-1/2 oz. pkg. spice cake mix
16-oz. can pumpkin
3/4 c. mayonnaise-type salad
   dressing

3 eggs, beaten
16-oz. container vanilla frosting
Garnish: red and green
   gumdrops, sliced

With an electric mixer on medium speed, beat together first
4 ingredients in a large bowl until well blended. Pour into a greased
15"x10" jelly-roll pan. Bake at 350 degrees for 18 to 20 minutes,
until edges pull away from sides of pan. Cool; spread with frosting
and cut into bars. Arrange a few sliced gumdrops on each bar to
resemble a holly sprig. Makes 3 dozen.

Use table linens or tea towels to wrap gifts...
the wrapping will be a lasting gift too.

Best-Ever **BAR COOKIES**

Chocolate-Caramel Pecan Bars

Gretchen Ohman
Troy, MI

For a spectacular dessert, make pecan bar sundaes. Cut into generous squares, then top each square with a scoop of vanilla ice cream, a drizzle of caramel and a sprinkle of pecans!

1-1/2 c. plus 3 T. all-purpose
  flour, divided
1/2 c. plus 2 T. butter, softened
  and divided
1/4 c. brown sugar, packed
3/4 c. caramel ice cream topping
3 eggs, beaten
3/4 c. light corn syrup
3/4 c. sugar
1 t. vanilla extract
12-oz. pkg. semi-sweet
  chocolate chips
1-1/2 c. chopped pecans

With an electric mixer on medium speed, mix together 1-1/2 cups flour, 1/2 cup butter and brown sugar until crumbly. Press into a greased 13"x9" baking pan. Bake at 350 degrees for 12 to 15 minutes, until golden; set aside. Combine caramel topping and remaining flour until mixture is fairly thick; set aside. Melt remaining butter; cool slightly. Whisk together eggs, corn syrup, sugar, melted butter and vanilla; stir in chocolate chips and pecans. Pour over baked crust; drizzle with caramel mixture. Bake for an additional 25 to 30 minutes. Cut into squares. Makes 2-1/2 dozen.

Arrange homebaked goodies
on a 3-tiered cake stand
for a delightful dessert tray
that doesn't take up much
space on a buffet.

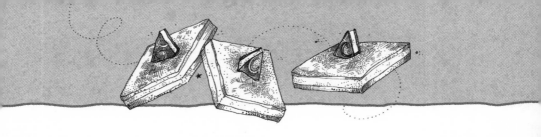

Heavenly Angel Bars

Susie Kadleck
San Antonio, TX

Just one bite and you will agree...these are truly heavenly!

16-oz. pkg. graham crackers, divided
1 c. sugar
3/4 c. milk, divided
1-1/2 c. margarine, divided
1-1/2 t. vanilla extract, divided
1 egg, beaten

1 c. sweetened flaked coconut
1 c. chopped pecans
8-oz. can crushed pineapple, drained
16-oz. pkg. powdered sugar
1/2 t. butter flavoring

Crush enough crackers to equal one cup; set aside. Combine sugar, 1/2 cup milk, one cup margarine, one teaspoon vanilla and egg in a saucepan over medium heat; bring to a boil. Remove from heat; add coconut, crushed crackers, pecans and pineapple. Line baking sheet with half of remaining whole crackers; spread warm mixture over top. Top with remaining whole crackers, arranged in same direction as bottom layer; set aside. Combine powdered sugar, butter flavoring, remaining margarine and remaining vanilla in a large bowl. Add enough of remaining milk to reach a spreading consistency, about 2 teaspoons at a time. Spread over top. Refrigerate for at least 2 hours before slicing along perforations of crackers. Makes 3 to 4 dozen.

If you have a child who's learning to bake, take a few minutes
to make copies of favorite family cookie recipes.
They'll be cherished years from now!

Old-Fashioned
COOKIES

Grandma's Baking Secrets

Measure flour carefully...too much can make cookies hard and dry. The amount of flour in a recipe can even be reduced by 1/4 cup to make extra-tender cookies.

✻

Use the type of fat named in the recipe...it's best not to substitute. Butter bakes up well and gives cookies wonderful flavor. Avoid light or whipped margarine. If shortening is called for, look for it in easy-to-measure sticks.

✻

Chill or freeze soft dough to make it easier to work with and help it hold its shape better. Cut-outs can even be chilled right on the baking sheet before baking.

✻

Use an oven thermometer to check baking temperatures... no more burnt or underdone cookies!

✻

When using dark baking sheets, lower the oven temperature by 25 degrees to avoid overbrowning.

✻

Set a kitchen timer...check cookies for doneness after the minimum baking time given.

Chocolate Thumbprints

Janice Gavarkavich
Martins Ferry, OH

*This cookie recipe I received from a friend. I have made
it for friends' weddings as well as for the holidays.
It is very simple and easy.*

16-oz. container chocolate
    frosting
1/4 c. butter, softened
2-1/2 c. graham cracker crumbs

1/2 t. almond extract
1 c. almonds, ground
48 milk chocolate drops,
    unwrapped

Combine frosting and butter in a large bowl; beat until well blended.
Stir in graham cracker crumbs and almond extract. Spread almonds
in a shallow bowl; set aside. Shape chocolate mixture into one-inch
balls; roll in ground almonds to coat. Place balls on ungreased baking
sheets. Make a deep thumbprint indentation in the center of each ball;
top with a chocolate drop. Refrigerate for 30 minutes, or until well
chilled. Makes 4 dozen.

No-bake cookies like Chocolate Thumbprints are perfect for children
just learning to cook...even the smallest child can press thumbprints
into the dough! Young cooks are sure to nibble on the dough, so you'll
want to select a recipe like this one that contains no eggs.

Grandmother's Springerle

Carol Lytle
Columbus, OH

*If you don't have a patterned wooden springerle pin, just score
rolled dough lightly into 2-inch squares. Stamp each
square with a new, floured rubber stamp.*

4 eggs
2 T. butter, softened
2 c. sugar
4 c. all-purpose flour

2 t. baking powder
1/4 t. salt
1/4 c. anise seed

Beat eggs in a large bowl until very light. Add butter and sugar; beat
until fluffy. Mix flour, baking powder and salt in another large bowl;
gradually add to butter mixture. Knead dough until smooth, adding
more flour if necessary. Cover and chill for at least 2 hours. Using a
plain rolling pin, roll out 1/2-inch thick on a lightly floured surface.
Roll again with a springerle rolling pin to make designs. Cut cookies
apart on lines marked by rolling pin. Sprinkle anise seed on a clean
tea towel; place cookies on towel, molded-side down. Let stand,
uncovered, overnight. Place cookies on lightly greased baking sheets.
Bake at 325 degrees for 12 to 15 minutes; cool completely. Store in
an airtight container. Cookies will gradually soften and develop
stronger anise flavor. Makes 5 dozen.

All during December, keep favorite Christmas books in a basket
that's close at hand when it's bedtime for little ones. Snuggle
together under a fuzzy blanket and read a story together...
what a special way to end the day!

Nanny's Pizzelles

Kelly Friedman
Bogota, NJ

Whenever I make these cookies, it brings me right back to my nanny's kitchen...I can taste her love in every bite. They always reminded us of snowflakes, even when we enjoyed them on hot summer days.

6 eggs, beaten
1-1/2 c. sugar
1 c. butter, melted
4 t. baking powder

2 T. anise extract
2 T. vanilla extract
3-1/2 c. all-purpose flour
Garnish: powdered sugar

Mix together all ingredients except flour and powdered sugar until creamy. Add flour gradually; mix well to make a very sticky dough. Drop dough by teaspoonfuls onto a hot pizzelle iron. Bake for 30 to 35 seconds until golden. Dust with powdered sugar. Makes about 5 dozen.

Make Chocolate Pizzelles! Omit the anise extract and add 1/2 cup baking cocoa, 1/2 cup sugar and 1/2 teaspoon baking powder to the ingredients above.

Dad's Favorite Date Sandwich Cookies

Heather Roberts
Quebec, Canada

This is our all-time favorite cookie! I remember helping my mom bake these when I was a little girl and still today I bake them for my family. I hope you enjoy making these. Try them with a cup of hot tea.

3 c. long-cooking oats, uncooked
2-1/2 c. all-purpose flour
1 t. baking powder
1/4 t. salt
2 c. brown sugar, packed and divided

1/2 c. margarine, melted
1/2 c. butter, melted
1/2 c. milk
16-oz. pkg. chopped dates
1 c. hot water

Mix together oats, flour, baking powder, salt, one cup brown sugar, margarine, butter and milk. Divide dough into 4 portions. On a floured surface, roll out one portion at a time to about 1/8-inch thick. Cut out shapes with a glass or round cookie cutter. Transfer to greased baking sheets. Bake at 325 degrees for 10 to 15 minutes. Remove to cool completely. To make filling, combine dates, remaining brown sugar and hot water over medium heat. Cook for 3 to 5 minutes, until thickened. Cool completely. Spread onto half of cookies; place another one on top. Makes 2 dozen large cookies or 3-1/2 dozen small cookies.

Wouldn't your family members just love to receive a tin of those special Christmas cookies or candies your grandmother always used to make?

Stella's Rugelach

Stella Hickman
Gooseberry Patch

*Since I'm diabetic, I was so pleased to find this cookie recipe that
uses sweetener instead of sugar. They are really yummy.*

1/2 c. chopped dates
1/2 c. pistachios, chopped
1/3 c. plus 2 T. powdered
   low-calorie sugar blend
   for baking, divided

3 t. cinnamon, divided
1/4 c. butter, softened
3 8-oz. tubes refrigerated
   crescent rolls

Combine dates, pistachios, 1/3 cup sugar blend, 2 teaspoons
cinnamon and butter in a medium bowl; mix well and set aside.
Separate crescent rolls. Spoon one teaspoon date mixture onto each
crescent roll; roll up. Arrange rolls on ungreased baking sheets. Bake
at 375 degrees for 13 to 18 minutes, until golden. Remove to a wire
rack. Combine remaining sugar blend and cinnamon; sprinkle over
cookies. Makes 2 dozen.

Kitchen shears are oh-so handy for cutting up
sticky dried fruit like dates and apricots.

121

Coconut Yule Logs

Alberta Wagy
San Diego, CA

Delightful bite-size morsels.

1-1/2 c. sweetened flaked
   coconut, divided
8-oz. pkg. cream cheese,
   softened
3 c. powdered sugar

1/2 t. vanilla extract
2 c. quick-cooking oats,
   uncooked
1/2 c. chopped almonds

Spread one cup coconut on a baking sheet. Bake at 325 degrees for 7 to 10 minutes, tossing occasionally, until toasted. Set aside to cool. Beat cream cheese in a large bowl until creamy. Gradually add powdered sugar, blending well; add vanilla. Stir in oats, remaining coconut and almonds. Shape to form 2-inch logs; roll logs in toasted coconut. Store in an airtight container; keep refrigerated until ready to serve. Makes 3 dozen.

Host a cookie sampling party! Have each friend bring a plate of her very best cookies, while you provide the coffee and tea. Take a vote on the tastiest, most beautiful and even the funniest cookies... hand out ribbons or little prizes. You'll have a ball together!

Holly Wreaths

Lori Harles
Franklin, OH

I found this recipe one day in my mother-in-law's recipe box...it sounded so quick & easy, I just had to try it. When I took a batch to work for our Christmas party, this was the first dessert to disappear!

1/2 c. butter	4-1/2 c. corn flake cereal
30 marshmallows	1/3 c. red cinnamon candies
1/4 to 1 t. green food coloring	

Melt butter in a large saucepan over low heat; add marshmallows and stir until melted. Add food coloring; mix well. Gently stir in cereal to coat well. Drop by teaspoonfuls onto greased aluminum foil; form into wreath shapes. Decorate with cinnamon candies for holly berries while still warm. Makes one to 1-1/2 dozen.

Whip up a mug of minty hot chocolate in a jiffy. Spoon 1/4 cup of chocolate chips into a mug, then pour in hot milk to fill mug. Stir with a peppermint stick until the chocolate melts...yum!

Almond Candy Canes

Zoe Bennett
Columbia, SC

*I like to tint the frosting pink with just a few drops
of red food coloring.*

1 c. butter, softened
2-1/2 c. powdered sugar,
　divided
1/4 t. salt
1 t. almond extract

1 c. chopped almonds
2 c. all-purpose flour
2 to 3 T. milk
4 to 6 candy canes, crushed

Combine butter, 1/2 cup powdered sugar, salt and extract in a large
bowl. With an electric mixer on medium-high speed, beat until fluffy.
Stir in almonds and flour until well blended. Roll dough by heaping
tablespoonfuls into a rope; shape into candy canes. Place on a
well-buttered or parchment paper-lined baking sheet. Bake at
350 degrees until lightly golden, about 15 to 17 minutes. Cool on
baking sheet until slightly firm; carefully remove to a wire rack and
cool completely. Stir together remaining powdered sugar and milk.
Drizzle frosting over cookies and sprinkle with crushed candy. Makes
about 2 dozen.

Clever gift tags in an instant...just trace around favorite
cookie cutters onto heavy paper and cut out.

St. Nick's Popcorn Balls

Sheri Dulaney
Englewood, OH

*These are so cute served on a platter! Tie strips of homespun
on the candy canes for a really festive look.*

5 qts. popped popcorn
2 c. sugar
1-1/2 c. water
1/2 t. salt

1/2 c. light corn syrup
1 t. vinegar
1 t. vanilla extract
15 to 20 candy canes

Place popped corn in a large roaster; keep warm and crisp in a
300-degree oven. Butter the inside of a medium saucepan; add
remaining ingredients except vanilla and candy canes. Cook to
hard-ball stage, 250 to 269 degrees on a candy thermometer; add
vanilla. Pour slowly over popped corn, stirring just enough to mix
thoroughly. Butter hands lightly; shape popcorn mixture into an
apple-size ball around straight end of each candy cane. Once cooled,
place balls candy cane-side up on a platter. Makes 15 to 20.

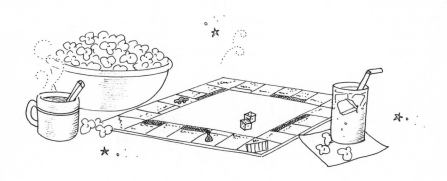

Need a gift for a special family? Give a board game or a couple of
card games along with a tin filled with homemade caramel corn...
it'll be much appreciated on the next snow day!

Date Pinwheels

Christine Gordon
Rapid City, SD

*A family favorite for Christmas...I like to make them
for any special occasion year 'round.*

16-oz. pkg. dates, chopped
1/2 c. water
1/2 c. sugar
1/2 t. vanilla extract
1 t. cinnamon, divided
1 c. butter-flavored shortening

2 c. brown sugar, packed
3 eggs
4 c. all-purpose flour
1 t. baking soda
1/2 t. salt

Combine dates, water and sugar in a medium saucepan over medium heat; cook until thickened. Stir in vanilla and 1/2 teaspoon cinnamon; cool. Combine shortening and brown sugar in a large bowl; add eggs, one at a time, beating well after each. In a separate large bowl, mix together flour, baking soda, salt and remaining cinnamon. Gradually add flour mixture to shortening mixture; stir well. Roll out half the dough to a 1/4-inch thick rectangle. Spread half of cooled date filling onto dough. Roll up jelly-roll style, starting at long end. Repeat with remaining dough and filling to make a second roll. Wrap rolls in plastic wrap; chill for 3 to 4 hours to overnight. Slice dough into 1/4-inch slices; arrange on greased baking sheets. Bake at 325 degrees for 10 to 12 minutes. Makes 6 dozen.

A nifty way to make perfectly shaped slice & bake cookies! Fill clean, empty small orange juice cans with dough and freeze. To bake, let thaw for 15 minutes, then remove bottom of can and push up dough. Cut dough across open end of can...ready to bake!

Polish Cookie Balls

Beverly Ray
Brandon, FL

Some folks call these Mexican Wedding Cakes or Russian Tea Cakes, but whatever you call them, they're delicious!

1 c. butter, softened
1/4 c. sugar
2 c. all-purpose flour

1 t. vanilla extract
1 c. pecans, finely chopped
1 c. powdered sugar

Combine butter, sugar, flour and vanilla in a large bowl until well blended; stir in pecans. Form into one-inch balls; arrange on ungreased baking sheets. Bake at 325 degrees for 20 to 25 minutes. Roll in powdered sugar while still hot. Makes about 2-1/2 dozen.

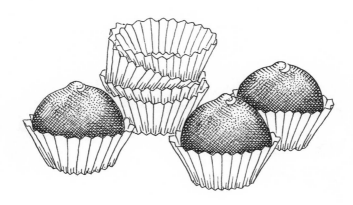

Someone special would love to receive their very own cookie & candy assortment. Tuck small round cookies and fudge truffles into mini paper muffin liners...arrange in separate compartments of a candy box. Sweet!

Almond Cream Spritz

Lisa Johnson
Hallsville, TX

Buttery and tender with a delicate almond flavor.

1 c. butter, softened
3-oz. pkg. cream cheese,
   softened
1/2 c. sugar

1/2 t. almond extract
1/4 t. vanilla extract
2 c. all-purpose flour
1/2 c. almonds, finely chopped

Beat together butter and cream cheese in a large mixing bowl until
well combined. Add sugar, almond extract and vanilla; mix well. Stir
in flour. Cover and chill dough for 30 minutes, or until easy to handle.
Place dough in a cookie press. Press out cookies onto ungreased
baking sheets; sprinkle with almonds. Bake at 375 degrees for 8 to
10 minutes, until edges of cookies are golden. Remove to wire racks
to cool. Makes 5 dozen.

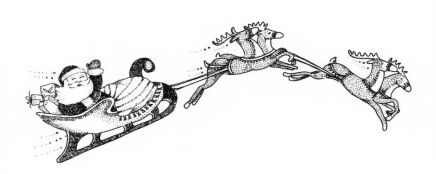

Be sure to let baking sheets cool between batches...a warm
baking sheet will cause dough to soften and spread.

Noels

April Hale
Kirkwood, NY

Bite into these tender cookies to find a hidden surprise...
a walnut inside a date!

1 lb. walnut halves
2 lbs. pitted whole dates
1/3 c. plus 2 T. butter, softened
    and divided
3/4 c. brown sugar, packed
1 egg, beaten
2 t. vanilla extract, divided

1-1/4 c. all-purpose flour
1/2 t. salt
1/2 t. baking soda
1/4 t. baking powder
1/2 c. plus 1 T. sour cream,
    divided
1 c. powdered sugar

Insert a walnut into each date; set aside. Combine 1/3 cup butter, brown sugar, egg, one teaspoon vanilla and flour; mix well. Stir in baking soda, baking powder and 1/2 cup sour cream. Dip dates in batter; arrange on lightly greased baking sheets. Bake at 350 degrees until lightly golden, about 3 to 4 minutes. Cool completely. Combine powdered sugar and remaining butter, vanilla and sour cream; spread on cookies. Makes about 3 dozen.

Coffee Eggnog

JoAnna Nicoline-Haughey
Berwyn, PA

Perfect for sipping at brunch.

1 qt. eggnog
3/4 c. coffee liqueur or cooled
    brewed coffee

Garnish: whipped topping,
    nutmeg

Combine eggnog and liqueur or coffee in a 1-1/2 quart pitcher. Pour into small cups. Top with whipped topping and sprinkle with nutmeg. Makes 8 servings.

Gingerbread Cottage

Nancy Wise
Little Rock, AR

It's become a tradition at our house for the kids to make these sweet little houses after Thanksgiving dinner has been cleared away. It's fun to see how creative the children can be!

1/2-pint empty milk carton, washed
Royal Icing
graham crackers, broken into squares

Garnish: mini candies, cereals, mini pretzels, sprinkles and other holiday treats
Optional: decorator frosting tubes

Secure milk carton to a square of cardboard with a dab of Royal Icing. Spread icing on sides of carton; press crackers firmly onto carton. Repeat for roof, using 2 crackers. For sides of roof, use a serrated knife to cut a cracker in half on the diagonal; press onto icing. Create windows and doors with desired garnishes, using icing to attach. Spread icing around house to look like snowdrifts. If desired, add accents with colored decorator frosting. Makes one cottage.

Royal Icing

Michelle Campen
Peoria, IL

This icing dries glossy and hard...perfect for decorating gingerbread houses or icing cookies that will be mailed.

1 pasteurized egg white

1-1/2 c. powdered sugar

Combine ingredients in a large bowl. Beat with an electric mixer on high speed until stiff peaks form. Makes about 3/4 cup.

Cinnamon Hard Candy

Linda Brown
Ocala, FL

Everyone loves this cheery red candy with its red-hot flavor! I like to fill small bags and tie with ribbons as gifts for co-workers.

1/2 c. powdered sugar	1 c. water
3-3/4 c. sugar	1 t. cinnamon flavoring
1-1/2 c. light corn syrup	1/2 to 1 t. red food coloring

Line a baking sheet with aluminum foil; sprinkle with powdered sugar and set aside. Combine sugar, corn syrup and water in a large saucepan over medium heat, stirring until sugar is dissolved. Bring mixture to a boil without stirring until it reaches the hard-crack stage, or 290 to 310 degrees on a candy thermometer. Stir in flavoring and food coloring. Pour hot candy onto prepared baking sheet. Let cool; break into pieces. Makes about 3 pounds.

Be creative...make hard candy in your favorite flavor, tinted to match! Try peppermint, lemon, cherry or butterscotch candy. Flavoring oils for candy making can be found in the supermarket baking aisle and at some drugstores too.

Fay's Candy Strawberries

Fay Melton
Sheffield, AL

*These berries look so sweet packed in green lattice
strawberry baskets! I save empty berry baskets
over the summer to present as gifts.*

2 3-oz. pkgs. strawberry
   gelatin mix
1/2 c. sweetened condensed
   milk
1 c. pecans, finely chopped

1 c. sweetened flaked coconut
1 t. vanilla extract
red and green decorating sugar
1/3 c. slivered almonds
few drops green food coloring

Beat together gelatin mixes and condensed milk in a large bowl until
smooth. Add pecans, coconut and vanilla; stir just until combined.
Shape into strawberries; roll sides of strawberries in red sugar and
dip tops into green sugar. Tint almonds with green food coloring and
insert one into the top of each berry for the stem. Store in an airtight
container in refrigerator. Makes 2 dozen.

Give a Christmas celebration in a bag! Slip holiday CD's,
ornaments and homemade cookies inside a festive
gift bag...that's sure to be a welcome hostess gift.

Sparkling Sugarplums

Rogene Rogers
Bemidji, MN

I wrap these candies individually in little squares of plastic wrap and tie them with gold cord. Then I arrange them in a fancy dish next to a note that reads, "While visions of sugarplums danced in their heads..."

1 c. dried apricots	2 c. vanilla wafers, crushed
1/2 c. pitted dates	1 c. sweetened flaked coconut
1/2 c. golden raisins	1/2 c. orange juice
1 c. pecans	1/2 c. sugar

Finely chop apricots, dates, raisins and pecans in a food processor. Combine with wafer crumbs in a large bowl; toss with coconut and orange juice. Form into 3/4-inch balls; roll in sugar and place in paper mini muffin liners. Makes about 4 dozen.

Just for fun, nestle Sparkling Sugarplums in the compartments of a festive red plastic ice cube tray.

Oh-So-Easy Cut-Outs

Jo Ann

The gel designs bake right into the cookies..no frosting mess!

17-1/2 oz. pkg. sugar
  cookie mix
2 T. all-purpose flour
1/3 c. butter, melted

1 egg, beaten
Garnish: decorator gel tubes in
  desired colors

Stir together cookie mix, flour, butter and egg. Chill briefly if very soft.
Roll dough out 1/4-inch thick on a lightly floured surface. Cut out
with cookie cutters. Place cookies one inch apart on ungreased baking
sheets. Decorate unbaked cookies with decorator gels. Bake at
375 degrees for 7 to 9 minutes, until lightly golden around edges.
Cool for one minute before removing from baking sheets; cool
completely. Makes 2 dozen.

Tuck a packet of fresh-baked cookies into a vintage
cookie jar...a fun gift for a new bride.

Italian Knot Cookies

Lynda Robson
Boston, MA

I was very happy when I found this recipe! The cookies turn out just like the ones my Italian grandmother used to make.

6 T. butter, softened	4 t. lemon juice
1/3 c. sugar	2 t. orange zest
1/2 t. salt	2 t. lemon zest
1/4 c. milk	1 t. rum extract
1 egg	2-1/2 c. all-purpose flour
1 egg yolk	oil for deep-frying
2 T. orange juice	Garnish: powdered sugar

Process butter, sugar and salt in a food processor until smooth. Add milk, egg, egg yolk, juices, zests and extract; process until smooth. Add flour; pulse until well combined. Turn dough out on a lightly floured surface; knead until soft but not sticky. Wrap in plastic wrap. Chill for at least 30 minutes, until dough is easy to handle. Divide dough in half. On a lightly floured surface, roll out one-half at a time into a 16-inch by 16-inch square. Using a fluted pastry cutter or a knife, cut dough into 10 strips, 1-1/2 inches wide. Cut strips in half crosswise. Tie each strip with a loose knot in the center; place on wax paper-lined baking sheets. Heat several inches of oil to 350 degrees in a large saucepan. Fry 6 to 8 knots at a time for 4 minutes, until golden, turning halfway through. Drain on paper towels; cool completely. Sprinkle with powdered sugar. Makes about 3-1/2 dozen.

Here's a thrifty old-fashioned tip...use clean brown paper grocery bags for draining deep-fried cookies..

Chocolate-Almond Fingers

Marlene Darnell
Newport Beach, CA

With 3 kinds of almonds, these shortbread fingers are delectable for dipping in coffee. Try bittersweet chocolate for a gourmet touch.

1/2 c. plus 2 T. butter, softened
   and divided
1 c. all-purpose flour
1/3 c. cornstarch
1/4 c. brown sugar, packed
1/3 c. almonds, ground

1 t. vanilla extract
1/4 t. almond extract
4 1-oz. sqs. semi-sweet baking
   chocolate, chopped
1/3 c. chopped almonds

Combine 1/2 cup butter, flour, cornstarch, brown sugar, ground almonds and extracts; mix until dough forms. Divide dough into 4 equal portions. Roll each portion into a 12 to 14-inch rope about 1/2-inch in diameter. Cut each rope into 2-inch lengths; arrange on ungreased baking sheets. Bake at 350 degrees for 18 to 20 minutes, just until golden on bottom. Cool on wire racks. Place chocolate in a microwave-safe container. Microwave on high setting for one to 1-1/2 minutes until melted; stir until smooth. Dip half of each cookie into melted chocolate, then into chopped almonds. Set on a wire rack over wax paper to harden. Makes about 2-1/2 dozen.

Oops, the cookies baked too long! If they're a little hard, but not burnt, slip a slice of fresh bread into the cookie jar overnight. Cookies will soften like magic.

Almond Sandies

Sharon Tillman
Hampton, VA

For a deliciously refreshing treat, substitute lemon extract for vanilla and assemble cookies in pairs with a spoonful of lemon curd.

3/4 c. sugar, divided
1/2 t. salt
3/4 c. almonds
1-1/2 c. butter, chopped and
  softened

4 t. vanilla extract
1/3 t. almond extract
3 c. all-purpose flour
3/4 c. coarse white or colored
  decorating sugar

Combine 1/2 cup sugar and salt in a food processor; process until very fine, about 30 to 60 seconds. Add almonds; process until finely chopped, about 20 seconds. Add butter and extracts; pulse until smooth. Add flour and pulse until a soft dough forms; spoon into a large bowl and mix well. Work in remaining sugar with a spoon. On a floured surface, shape dough into 3 logs, each 6 inches long by 1-3/4 inches in diameter. Wrap in wax paper; refrigerate for at least 2 hours. Spread coarse sugar evenly over a flat surface. Roll dough logs in sugar to coat well. Slice logs 1/4-inch thick; arrange one inch apart on ungreased baking sheets. Bake at 350 degrees for 12 to 15 minutes. Let stand on baking sheets for 2 minutes; transfer to a wire rack to cool completely. Keep stored in an airtight container. Makes about 6 dozen.

Cinnamon-Sugar Pinwheels

Kay Jones
Cleburne, TX

The filling reminds us of Grandma's cinnamon toast.

1/2 c. butter, softened
3-oz. pkg. cream cheese,
  softened
1 egg yolk
1 c. all-purpose flour
1/4 c. butter, melted

1/3 c. sugar
2 t. cinnamon
1/2 c. nuts, finely chopped
Garnish: powdered sugar

Combine butter and cream cheese; blend until smooth. Stir in egg yolk and flour; mix well. Cover and chill for 30 minutes. Divide dough in half; roll very thin, about 1/8-inch thick. Brush with melted butter; set aside. Combine sugar, cinnamon and nuts; sprinkle over dough. Roll up jelly-roll style, beginning at long edge. Slice rolls into 1/2-inch slices; arrange on ungreased baking sheets. Repeat with remaining dough. Bake at 350 degrees for 15 minutes, or until golden. Remove to wire rack and cool; sprinkle with powdered sugar. Makes 2-1/2 to 3 dozen.

Turn Cinnamon-Sugar Pinwheels into cookie pops...easy! Join 2 cookies with frosting, placing a treat stick in between. Wrap in colorful cellophane and tie with curling ribbon.

Pastel Cream Wafers

Vickie

*I like to use a small scallop-edged round cutter
for these dainty wafers.*

2 c. all-purpose flour
1-1/2 c. butter, divided
1/3 c. whipping cream
2 c. sugar

2-1/3 c. powdered sugar
1 t. vanilla extract
several drops red food coloring

Combine flour, one cup butter and cream; mix well. Chill for one hour.
Roll out dough to 1/8-inch thick; cut out cookies with a 1-1/2 inch
round cookie cutter. Carefully dip both sides of cookies into sugar;
place on a parchment paper-lined baking sheet. Pierce cookies lightly
across top with a fork. Bake at 375 degrees for 7 to 9 minutes. Cool
completely. Beat remaining butter for 30 seconds; gradually beat in
powdered sugar, vanilla and food coloring. Sandwich cookies in pairs
with frosting. Makes about 5 dozen.

An instant table decoration! Arrange holiday cookies around
the base of a glass hurricane for an edible wreath.

Two-Tone Icebox Cookies

Mary Murray
Gooseberry Patch

*Five kinds of cookies from one dough recipe...amazing! Just
follow directions on these two pages for shaping dough
into bull's eyes, pinwheels, logs or checkerboard cookies.*

1 c. butter, softened
1 c. sugar
1 egg
1 egg yolk

1 t. vanilla extract
2-3/4 c. all-purpose flour
2 T. baking cocoa

In a large bowl, blend together butter and sugar. Beat in egg, yolk and
vanilla. Gradually add flour. Divide dough into 2 equal portions. Beat
cocoa into one portion. Form dough into 2 rolls. Wrap dough in plastic
wrap; refrigerate for at least 4 hours. Cut into 1/4-inch slices; arrange
one inch apart on lightly greased baking sheets. Bake at
350 degrees for 8 to 10 minutes. Makes 2 dozen.

Bull's Eye Cookies:

Wrap a dough rectangle of one color around a dough log of another
color. It's fun to make half the cookies with dark dough centers, the
other half with light dough centers. Follow directions above for
refrigerating dough, slicing and baking.

Rescue dry, crumbly cookie
dough by adding a little
milk, one tablespoon
at a time.

More Two-Tone Variations

Checkerboard Cookies:

Form each roll of dough into 2 long, thin ropes, to equal 4 ropes. Press one light rope and one dark rope together; repeat with remaining 2 ropes. Place one pair of ropes on top of the other, alternating light and dark doughs. Press ropes together to form a long roll; repeat with remaining dough. Follow directions at left for refrigerating dough, slicing and baking.

Pinwheel Cookies:

To make these, layer 2 rectangles of different colored doughs together, then roll them up in a log shape. Follow directions at left for refrigerating dough, slicing and baking.

Almond Logs:

Follow directions at left for refrigerating dough. Roll chilled dough into 1/2-inch thick ropes and cut into 2-inch lengths. Dip each log into beaten egg white, then into chopped or sliced almonds. Follow baking directions at left.

Jam Turnovers

Nancy Girard
Chesapeake, VA

*Choose your favorite jam for the filling in these little pies.
Drizzle them with white icing for a pretty finish.*

3-oz. pkg. cream cheese
1/2 c. butter, softened
1 c. all-purpose flour

1/8 t. salt
12-oz. jar red raspberry jam or
   preserves

Blend cream cheese and butter together; stir in flour and salt. Roll out on a floured surface. Cut out circles with a 2-inch round cookie cutter. Place a teaspoonful of jam or preserves in the center of each circle. Fold over and press edges together with a fork to seal well. Place on ungreased baking sheets. Bake at 375 degrees for 10 to 15 minutes. Makes 16 to 20.

Wrapped in love! Use children's drawings as wrapping paper for gifts from the kitchen. Perfect for grandparents and aunts & uncles.

Viennese Crescents

Rhonda Reeder
Ellicott City, MD

We're lucky to have a hazelnut tree in our yard,
but you can substitute almonds for the hazelnuts.

2 c. all-purpose flour
1 c. butter, softened
1 c. hazelnuts, ground
2-1/2 c. powdered sugar,
　divided

1/8 t. salt
1 t. vanilla extract
1 T. vanilla-flavored powdered
　non-dairy creamer

Combine flour, butter, nuts, 1/2 cup powdered sugar, salt and vanilla.
Mix by hand until well blended. Cover and chill for one hour. Shape
dough into one-inch balls; roll each ball into a small roll 3 inches long
and curve to form a crescent shape. Place 2 inches apart on ungreased
baking sheets. Bake at 375 degrees for 10 to 12 minutes, or until
golden and set. Let stand for one minute; remove from cookie sheets.
Mix remaining powdered sugar and creamer. Sprinkle hot cookies with
powdered sugar mixture; turn gently to coat on both sides. Cool and
store in airtight container. Makes 2 dozen.

Découpage Grandma's favorite Christmas cookie recipe onto the
lid of a tin and fill with fresh-baked cookies...sweet!

Golden Tassies

Beverly Ray
Brandon, FL

Dress up these tiny tarts for the holidays. Use a mini cookie cutter to cut out tiny stars or hearts from leftover dough. Place cut-outs on top of filling before baking.

1 c. margarine, softened
2 3-oz. pkgs. cream cheese, softened
2 c. all-purpose flour
1 c. pecans, finely chopped and divided

3 eggs, beaten
3 T. margarine, melted
2-1/4 c. brown sugar, packed
2 t. vanilla extract
1/2 t. salt

Mix together softened margarine and cream cheese; gradually add flour. Mix well; refrigerate for 30 minutes or longer. Press one-inch balls of dough into ungreased mini muffin tins, shaping with floured fingers. Sprinkle about one teaspoon chopped pecans into each muffin cup. Combine eggs, melted margarine, brown sugar, vanilla and salt, beating until smooth. Pour over nuts. Sprinkle remaining nuts over top. Bake at 325 degrees for 25 to 30 minutes. Makes 3 to 4 dozen.

Toss together a festive snack mix from baking ingredients already on hand. Simply combine equal amounts of honey-roasted peanuts, sweetened dried cranberries and white chocolate chips. Pour into your prettiest dish and surprise guests!

Caramel-Coffee Tassies

Staci Meyers
Ideal, GA

In a word...delectable!

3-oz. pkg. cream cheese,
   softened
1/2 c. butter, softened
1 c. all-purpose flour
14-oz. pkg. caramels,
   unwrapped

1/4 c. evaporated milk
1-1/2 t. coffee liqueur or brewed
   coffee

Beat cream cheese and butter together until well blended; stir in flour. Form into a ball; chill for one hour to overnight. Shape dough into 1/2-inch balls; press each into a ungreased mini muffin tin. Bake at 350 degrees for 10 to 15 minutes, until golden. Let cool. Combine caramels and evaporated milk in a saucepan over medium heat. Stir frequently until melted. Remove from heat; stir in liqueur or coffee. Spoon caramel filling into baked shells; let cool. Pipe frosting onto caramel filling. Makes about 2 dozen.

Frosting:

1 c. shortening
2/3 c. sugar
2/3 c. evaporated milk, chilled

1 t. coffee liqueur or brewed
   coffee

Blend shortening and sugar together until fluffy; add evaporated milk and liqueur or coffee. Beat with an electric mixer on medium-high until fluffy, about 7 to 10 minutes.

Grandmother's Butter Fingers

Janice Miller
Huntington, IN

*My family delivers cookies to people that have to work on
Christmas Day. These cookies are always requested!*

1 c. chopped pecans
2-1/2 c. all-purpose flour
3/4 c. sugar

1 c. butter, softened
1 t. vanilla extract
16-oz. pkg. powdered sugar

Combine all ingredients except powdered sugar and mix well. Form
dough into small fingers or logs; place on an ungreased baking sheet.
Bake at 325 degrees for 20 to 30 minutes. Immediately roll in
powdered sugar to coat. Makes about 8 dozen.

On Christmas Eve, don't forget to leave out cookies & milk for Santa.
Treat the kids to cookies before bedtime too!

Peppermint Biscotti

Marian Buckley
Fontana, CA

*Be sure to select peppermint extract, not spearmint,
for that candy cane flavor.*

3/4 c. butter, softened
3/4 c. sugar
3 eggs
2 t. peppermint extract
3-1/4 c. all-purpose flour
1 t. baking powder

1/4 t. salt
1-1/2 c. candy canes, crushed
   and divided
2 c. semi-sweet chocolate chips
2 T. shortening

Blend butter and sugar. Add eggs, one at a time, beating well after each addition; stir in extract. Combine flour, baking powder, salt and one cup crushed candy in a separate bowl. Gradually add flour mixture to butter mixture, mixing well to a stiff dough. Divide dough in half. Roll each half into a 12-inch by 2-1/2 inch rectangle; place on ungreased baking sheets. Bake at 350 degrees for 25 to 30 minutes, until golden. Carefully remove to wire racks; cool for 15 minutes. Transfer to a cutting board; with a sharp knife, slice 1/2-inch thick on the diagonal. Return slices to baking sheets, cut-side down. Bake an additional 12 to 15 minutes, until firm. Cool on wire racks. In a microwave-safe bowl, melt chocolate chips and shortening; stir until smooth. Dip one end of each cookie into melted chocolate; roll in remaining crushed candy. Place on wax paper until set. Store in an airtight container. Makes about 3-1/2 dozen.

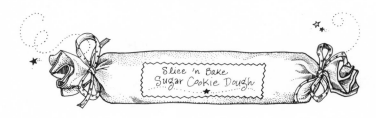

Slice 'n Bake
Sugar Cookie Dough

Such a thoughtful gift for a busy mom! Wrap up a roll of sugar cookie dough along with fun decorations...colorful sprinkles, candy-coated chocolates and of course a cookie cutter or two. She'll love it!

French Madeleines

Beth Kramer
Port Saint Lucie, FL

These delicate seashell-shaped cookies are perfect for a tea tray.

2 eggs, beaten
1/2 t. vanilla extract
1/2 t. lemon zest
1 c. powdered sugar

3/4 c. all-purpose flour
1/4 t. baking powder
1/2 c. butter, melted and cooled
Garnish: powdered sugar

Beat eggs, vanilla and lemon zest for 5 minutes with an electric mixer on high speed. Gradually add powdered sugar. Beat for 5 to 7 minutes, until thick and glossy; set aside. Stir together flour and baking powder. Add 1/4 of flour mixture to egg mixture and gently fold in with a spoon; gradually fold in remaining flour. Stir in butter. Spoon batter into 24 greased and floured 3-inch madeleine molds, filling 3/4 full. Bake at 375 degrees for 10 to 12 minutes, until edges are golden. Place molds on a rack to cool for one minute. Loosen edges with a knife; turn out cookies onto a wire rack to cool. Sprinkle with powdered sugar. Keep stored in an airtight container. Makes 2 dozen.

Treat yourself to just-baked goodness...wrap two cookies in a paper
towel and microwave on high setting for 30 to 45 minutes.
Mmm...don't forget a glass of icy cold milk!

Raspberry Linzer Tarts

Cathy Hillier
Salt Lake City, UT

Speed up preparation of these dainty cookies by purchasing almonds already ground...they're also labeled as almond meal.

1-1/4 c. butter, softened
2/3 c. sugar
1-3/4 c. almonds, ground
1/8 t. cinnamon

2 c. all-purpose flour
6 T. raspberry jam
Garnish: powdered sugar

Blend butter and sugar until light and fluffy. Stir in almonds, cinnamon and flour, 1/2 cup at a time. Cover and refrigerate for about one hour. On a lightly floured surface, roll out half of dough 1/8-inch thick. Cut out 24 circles with a 2-1/2 inch round cookie cutter. Cut out centers of 12 circles with a 1/2-inch mini cookie cutter; leave remaining 12 circles uncut. Arrange one inch apart on ungreased baking sheets. Bake at 325 degrees for 10 to 15 minutes, until golden. Cool completely on a wire rack. Spread jam thinly over solid circles; sandwich each with a cut-out cookie. Spoon a little of remaining jam into cut-outs; sprinkle with powdered sugar. Makes one dozen.

A very special gift for a young lady! Line an old-fashioned hatbox with an eyelet-edged tea towel and add cookies, a packet of spiced teabags and a dainty teacup & saucer set.

Cream-Filled Pecan Snaps

Claire Bertram
Lexington, KY

*Cookies may begin to set before shaping. If so, simply pop
back in the oven for a minute to soften.*

3 T. butter, melted
1/4 c. brown sugar, packed
2 T. dark corn syrup
1 T. coffee liqueur or brewed
    coffee
1/2 c. pecans, finely chopped

1/4 c. all-purpose flour
1 c. whipping cream
1/4 c. powdered sugar
4 t. instant espresso coffee
Optional: grated chocolate

Combine butter, brown sugar, corn syrup and coffee liqueur or coffee
in a small bowl. Stir in pecans and flour until combined. Drop onto
lightly greased baking sheets by tablespoonfuls, 5 inches apart. Bake
at 350 degrees for 8 to 10 minutes, until bubbly and golden. Cool on
baking sheets for one to 2 minutes. Quickly roll each cookie around a
metal cone or a wooden spoon handle; slide off. Cool completely on a
wire rack. Shortly before serving, combine cream, powdered sugar and
espresso powder. Beat with an electric mixer on low speed until stiff
peaks form. Spoon into a plastic zipping bag; snip off one corner and
pipe into cookies. Dust with grated chocolate, if desired. Makes about
2-1/2 dozen.

Tuck a vintage milk bottle filled with creamy eggnog into
a gift basket of homebaked cookies. Tie on a nutmeg
grater and a whole nutmeg for extra flavor.

TREATS IN A
Twinkle

Share the Cookies, Share the Joy!

Host a cookie swap...a terrific way to get a great variety of
Christmas cookies without much effort! Invite 6 to 8 friends
and let them know how many dozen cookies to bring
(a dozen cookies for each guest).

° ❄ °

Invite a young friend to bake with you. Whether you're a
basic baker or a master chef, you're sure to have fun
as you measure, stir and sample together.

° ❄ °

Dig into Grandma's recipe box for that extra-special cookie
you remember...and then bake some to share with the whole
family. (If you don't have her recipe box, maybe you'll spot
that same recipe in a Gooseberry Patch cookbook!)

° ❄ °

Host a dessert open house for friends & neighbors instead
of an elaborate holiday party. Serve lots of cookies with coffee,
tea and festive mulled cider or hot cocoa...just add fun and
fellowship for a delightful no-stress afternoon!

° ❄ °

Set aside a dozen cookies from each batch you bake. In no time
at all, you can make up several platters of assorted cookies to
drop off at a neighborhood firehouse, emergency room, family
shelter or retirement home. They're sure to be much appreciated.

Pecan Icebox Cookies

Lisa Green
Parkersburg, WV

*For years these have been my family's special cookies for
Christmas...they're always the first ones to be eaten up!*

1-1/2 c. butter, softened
1 c. sugar
1 c. brown sugar, packed
2 eggs, beaten
1 t. baking soda

2 t. vanilla extract
1/8 t. salt
4 c. all-purpose flour
1 t. cream of tartar
1 c. chopped pecans

Mix together butter, sugars and eggs until creamy. Add remaining
ingredients except pecans; mix well. Stir in pecans and form into 3 to
4 logs 2 inches wide. Roll each log in wax paper, covering well;
chill for one hour to overnight. Slice 1/4-inch thick and arrange on
ungreased baking sheets. Bake at 350 degrees for 8 to 10 minutes.
Makes 7 to 8 dozen.

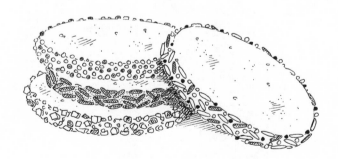

Dress up icebox cookies for the holidays! Simply roll logs of
chilled dough in colored sugar before slicing and baking.

Chocolate Cherry Delights

Maureen Erickson
Everett, WA

Here's another must-make recipe for Christmas...I got it a few years ago from my sister-in-law. It's a no-bake treat.

1/4 c. butter, melted
2 c. powdered sugar
12 maraschino cherries, finely chopped
2/3 c. creamy peanut butter
1 c. chopped walnuts

1 c. sweetened flaked coconut
1/8 t. salt
6-oz. pkg. semi-sweet chocolate chips
3-1/2 T. paraffin, chopped

Mix together all ingredients except chocolate chips and paraffin. Form into one-inch balls; set aside. Melt chocolate chips and paraffin in a double boiler over medium-low heat until smooth. Dip balls into chocolate mixture to coat; let stand on wax paper until set. Makes about 2-1/2 dozen.

...if it is going to be our kind of Christmas,
most of the presents will be homemade.

-Robert Tristram Coffin

Devil's Food Cookies

Barb Traxler
Mankato, MN

Here's a new favorite recipe of mine. Even children can make these cookies with a little help from an adult.

18-1/2 oz. pkg. devil's food
  cake mix
1 egg, beaten
3/4 c. chopped pecans or
  walnuts

12-oz. container frozen whipped
  topping, thawed
Garnish: powdered sugar

Combine all ingredients except powdered sugar in a large bowl; mix well. Form into one-inch balls; roll in powdered sugar. Bake at 350 degrees on an ungreased baking sheet for 10 to 12 minutes. Makes 4 dozen.

Pick up some paintable wooden cut-outs in holiday shapes at a neighborhood craft store. They're fun and easy for kids to decorate as package tie-ons that can later be used as tree ornaments.

Oatmeal Drop Cookies

Marion Marosevitch
White Haven, PA

*When the kids are young and eager to help, you may find
the cookies disappearing before they even reach
the wax paper to firm up!*

2 c. sugar
1/4 c. baking cocoa
1/2 c. milk
1/2 c. margarine
3 c. quick-cooking oats,
   uncooked

1/4 c. creamy peanut butter
1 t. vanilla extract
1/8 t. salt

Combine sugar, cocoa, milk and margarine in a large saucepan over
medium heat. Bring to a boil; cook for one minute. Remove from heat
and add oats, peanut butter, vanilla and salt; mix well. Drop mixture
by teaspoonfuls onto wax paper. Let stand for 2 to 3 hours. Makes
about 5 dozen.

Tag-sale baskets are wonderful for delivering homemade holiday
cookies. Simply line with a festive napkin, tie a satin bow
and a few jingle bells on the handle and it's ready to go!

Peanut Butter Pinwheels

Andrea Ballard
Jacksonville, AR

My mother-in-law makes these adorable treats at Christmastime.
They simply melt in your mouth...and taste like they
take a lot longer to make than they really do!

1 c. butter, softened
16-oz. pkg. powdered sugar
additional powdered sugar for
   rolling out

1 c. creamy peanut butter

Combine butter and powdered sugar until well mixed. Divide mixture into 3 balls. Using a rolling pin sprinkled with powdered sugar, roll out each ball into an 1/8-thick rectangle on wax paper sprinkled with powdered sugar. Spread a thin layer of peanut butter on top. Starting with long side of each rectangle, roll up jelly-roll style. Refrigerate for at least 30 minutes; slice 3/4-inch thick. Makes about 2-1/2 dozen.

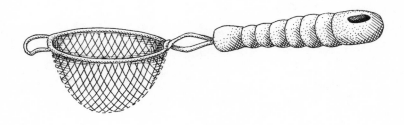

A tea strainer makes short work of sifting
powdered sugar over baked cookies.

Corny Crunch Bars

Jeannine Mertz
Hurdsfield, ND

If you like sweet & salty treats, you'll love these bars!

2 c. light corn syrup
2 c. sugar

2 c. crunchy peanut butter
2 9-3/4 oz. pkgs corn chips

Combine corn syrup and sugar in a saucepan over medium heat; bring to a boil. Remove from heat; stir in peanut butter. Place corn chips in a large bowl coated with non-stick vegetable spray; stir in peanut butter mixture. Gently press onto a buttered 18"x12" baking pan and let cool. Slice into squares. Makes about 2 dozen.

Make a gift card extra special...tie the holder to the
handle of a goodie-filled take-out container!

Marbled Cheesecake Bars

Lori Fehr
Alberta, Canada

These are so fast, easy and yummy you'll make them often.
They freeze well too....if you have any left!

18-3/4 oz. pkg. German
   chocolate cake mix
8-oz. pkg. cream cheese,
   softened

1/2 c. sugar
3/4 c. milk chocolate chips,
   divided

Prepare cake mix according to package directions; pour into a greased 17"x12" baking pan and set aside. Beat cream cheese and sugar together; stir in 1/4 cup chocolate chips. Drop by tablespoonfuls over batter. Cut through batter with a knife to swirl cream cheese mixture; sprinkle with remaining chocolate chips. Bake at 350 degrees for 25 to 30 minutes, or until a toothpick inserted near center tests clean. Cool on a wire rack; slice into bars. Makes about 3 dozen.

Any aspiring young baker would love to have her very own baking tools. Fill an unbreakable batter bowl with a wire whisk, measuring cups & spoons, an oven mitt and of course a cookbook...a gift that's sure to please!

Peanut Butter Snowballs

Marcia Reps
Utica, MN

Sprinkle with sparkling coarse sugar crystals for an icy finish.

2 c. creamy peanut butter
2 T. butter, softened
2 c. powdered sugar

2 c. crispy rice cereal
16-oz. pkg. white melting
   chocolate, chopped

Blend peanut butter, butter and powdered sugar. Add cereal; mix well.
Shape into balls by teaspoonfuls. Set balls on wax paper; freeze for
several hours to overnight. Melt chocolate in a double boiler over
medium-low heat; stir until smooth. Dip balls into melted chocolate;
return to wax paper until set. Makes 4 to 5 dozen.

Keep a candy-dipping tool on hand...it makes child's play of creating
the most delectable chocolate-dipped cookies and truffles!

Merry Christmas Cookies

Maria McGovern
Stratford, NJ

*An easy tried & true recipe that I like to use
for holiday cookie swaps.*

2 16-1/2 oz. tubes refrigerated
   sugar cookie dough,
   softened
1 c. dried cherries, chopped

1 c. pistachios, chopped
2 11-oz. pkgs. white chocolate
   chips

Combine cookie dough, cherries and pistachios in a large bowl; mix well. Shape into 2 logs; chill for one hour. Slice cookies 1/4-inch thick; arrange on lightly greased baking sheets. Bake at 350 degrees for 12 to 14 minutes, until golden. Cool completely. Melt chocolate in a double boiler over medium-low heat; stir until smooth. Dip cookies in melted chocolate and place on wax paper; let stand until set. Makes about 5 dozen.

In a hurry? Instead of frosting, simply top cookies with a few chocolate chips as soon as they come out of the oven. The chocolate will soften quickly and can be spread with a small spatula. Toss on a few candy sprinkles...done!

Pecan Pie Bars

Phyllis Drew
Madison, SD

Delectable...and it's my little secret how easy they are to make!

18-1/2 oz. pkg. yellow cake
   mix, divided
1/2 c. butter, melted
1 egg, beaten
1/2 c. brown sugar, packed

1-1/2 c. light corn syrup
3 eggs, beaten
1 t. vanilla extract
1 c. chopped pecans

Set aside 2/3 cup dry cake mix for filling. In a large bowl, combine remaining cake mix, butter and egg; mix well. Press into a greased 13"x9" baking pan. Bake at 350 degrees for 15 to 20 minutes, until lightly golden; remove and set aside. In a large bowl, combine reserved cake mix, brown sugar, corn syrup, eggs and vanilla. Beat for 2 minutes with an electric mixer on medium speed. Stir in pecans and pour over baked crust. Bake for 30 to 35 minutes at 350 degrees, until almost set. Cool; slice into bars. Makes about 2 dozen.

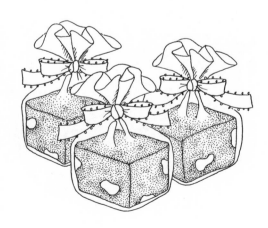

Oversize cookie bars are tempting, but for a change, slice them
into one-inch squares. Guests will feel free to try
"just a bite" of several different treats.

TREATS IN A Twinkle

Gingerbread Pinwheels

Elizabeth Blackstone
Racine, WI

Sprinkle with coarse white sanding sugar before baking.

16-1/2 oz. tube refrigerated
gingerbread cookie dough,
halved lengthwise

16-1/2 oz. tube refrigerated
sugar cookie dough, halved
lengthwise

Place gingerbread dough halves side-by-side on a wax paper-lined 15"x10" jelly-roll pan. Roll or pat into a single 15-inch by 9-inch rectangle; freeze for 5 minutes. Repeat steps with sugar cookie dough. Lifting with wax paper on bottom, turn over sugar cookie dough and lay on top of gingerbread dough. Gently pat doughs together; refrigerate 15 minutes. Peel off wax paper on top. Starting with one long side, roll up stacked dough jelly-roll style, peeling off bottom wax paper as dough is rolled. Wrap tightly in more wax paper; freeze for 45 minutes. Unwrap dough and slice 1/4-inch thick. Arrange slices 2 inches apart on ungreased baking sheets. Bake at 350 degrees for 10 to 12 minutes. Makes 4-1/2 dozen.

For a quick & easy wrap, set a tin of cookies in the center of a holiday-print fabric napkin. Gather the napkin up around the tin and secure with a bow...tie on a little bell just for fun!

Chewy Cereal Bars

Amy Curtis
Osage City, KS

*Try fruit-flavored cereal rings for a fun, colorful version or
make a nutritious treat with multi-grain cereal rings.*

1 c. sugar
1 c. light corn syrup
1 c. creamy peanut butter

1 t. vanilla extract
6 c. doughnut-shaped oat cereal

Stir together sugar and corn syrup in a saucepan over medium heat;
boil for one minute. Remove from heat; add peanut butter and vanilla,
stirring until smooth. Place cereal in a large bowl coated with
non-stick cooking spray; stir in peanut butter mixture. Press into a
buttered 15"x10" jelly roll pan and let cool. Slice into squares. Makes
2 to 2-1/2 dozen.

Pop up a big bowl of fresh popcorn on baking day...the kids (and you!)
will have something tasty to nibble on, saving the nuts and
chocolate chips for the cookies.

Club Cracker Goodie Bars

Jackie Balla
Walbridge, OH

My mother-in-law shared this recipe with me.
These easy no-bake bars are delicious!

60 rectangular buttery crackers,
    divided
1/2 c. butter
1/3 c. milk
1/2 c. sugar

3/4 c. brown sugar, packed
1 c. graham cracker crumbs
1 c. semi-sweet chocolate chips
2/3 c. crunchy peanut butter
1/2 c. chopped peanuts

In a lightly greased 13"x9" baking pan, arrange half of crackers in a single layer; set aside. Melt butter in a saucepan over medium heat; add milk, sugars and graham cracker crumbs. Boil for 5 minutes; pour over crackers in pan. Top with remaining crackers. Melt chocolate chips and peanut butter in a saucepan over low heat, stirring constantly until melted; spread over crackers. Sprinkle with peanuts. Cover and refrigerate for 3 hours. Slice into bars; refrigerate until ready to serve. Makes about 2-1/2 dozen.

Tuck a package of cookies into a red & white plush
Santa hat for a whimsical gift.

Terry's Butter Brickle Cookies

Terry Lee
Waverly, TN

Most requested at church socials...yummy!

18-oz. pkg. butter pecan cake
   mix
2 eggs, beaten

1/2 c. margarine, softened
8-oz. pkg. toffee baking bits

Mix together all ingredients. Drop by tablespoonfuls onto greased baking sheets. Bake at 350 degrees for 9 to 10 minutes. Makes 3-1/2 to 4 dozen.

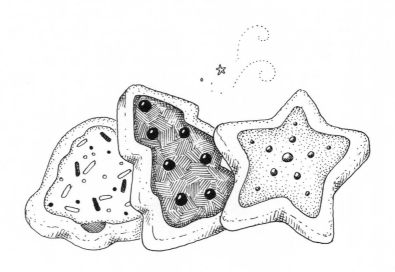

Remember to ask the kids when selecting cookie recipes
to bake for Christmas...there may just be a secret favorite
or two that will make the holiday complete!

Easy Almond Spritz

Diana Chaney
Olathe, KS

Make a whole tray of cookies in different colors and shapes from one batch of dough! Just divide dough into several portions, tint each a different color and press out using various cookie press shapes.

17-1/2 oz. pkg. sugar cookie
  mix
1/2 c. butter, melted
1 egg, beaten

1/2 c. all-purpose flour
1 t. almond extract
Garnish: colored sugar, candy
  sprinkles

In a large bowl, stir together dry cookie mix, butter, egg, flour and extract until a soft dough forms. Fill a cookie press with cookie dough; press cookies onto ungreased baking sheets. Decorate as desired with sugar or sprinkles. Bake at 375 degrees for 6 to 8 minutes, or until set. Cool for one minute; remove from baking sheets to wire rack. Makes 4 dozen.

When decorating with candy sprinkles, cover the table first with a length of parchment or wax paper. Return any excess sprinkles to their jars by simply folding the paper in half, gently shaking sprinkles to one side and tilting them into the jar.

Peanut Butter Meltaways

Tammy Smith
Avonmore, PA

A real favorite! All our holiday visitors ask,
"Did you make the Meltaways?"

8 1-oz. sqs. melting chocolate
8 1-oz. sqs. white melting
  chocolate

1 T. shortening
2-1/4 c. creamy peanut butter

Line a 13"x9" baking pan with aluminum foil; spray with non-stick vegetable spray and set aside. In a large microwave-safe bowl, combine chocolates and shortening. Microwave on high setting for 30 seconds at a time until melted; stir until smooth. Add peanut butter to chocolate mixture and stir well. Pour into prepared pan; chill for one hour. Cut into squares. Makes 2 dozen.

Easiest-ever Christmas bark...melt white melting chocolate
in the microwave. Stir in chopped candy canes, pour onto
wax paper to chill, then break into pieces.

Graham Kringles

Sandi Boothman
Camden, MI

A friend gave me this recipe...it's wonderful for the holidays.

24 cinnamon graham cracker
  squares
1/2 c. margarine

1/2 c. butter
1 c. brown sugar, packed
1 c. chopped pecans

Layer graham crackers in an aluminum foil-lined 15"x10" jelly-roll pan. Melt margarine, butter and brown sugar in a saucepan over medium heat. Bring to a boil; simmer for 2 minutes. Pour over crackers; sprinkle with nuts. Bake at 350 degrees for 10 to 12 minutes. Slice into triangles while still warm. Makes 4 dozen.

Use a baby spoon to help control the amount of
colored sugar that's added.

Angel Meringues

April Jacobs
Loveland, CO

Sugar-free and light as a feather!

5 egg whites
1/3 c. powdered calorie-free
  sweetener

1-1/2 t. vanilla extract
1/8 t. salt

With an electric mixer on medium-low speed, beat egg whites until frothy. Add sweetener, vanilla and salt. Mix on high speed until stiff peaks form, about 20 to 30 seconds. Spoon by rounded tablespoon-fuls onto a lightly greased baking sheet. Bake at 350 degrees for 10 to 15 minutes, until golden. Remove from pan; cool. Makes about one dozen.

For fancy Angel Meringues worthy of displaying on a tea tray, tint pale pink with a few drops of red food coloring. Spoon into a pastry tube with a large star decorating tip and pipe onto baking sheet.

TREATS IN A Twinkle

Flo's Santa Cookies

Flo Burtnett
Gage, OK

Kids just love these!

1 c. powdered sugar
2 T. milk
1/2 t. vanilla extract
16-oz. pkg. peanut-shaped
  sandwich cookies
4-1/4 oz. tube red decorator
  icing

Garnish: quartered mini marshmallows, mini semi-sweet
  chocolate chips, red
  cinnamon candies

Mix powdered sugar, milk and vanilla together to a frosting
consistency. Spread a small amount of frosting on each end of
cookies, leaving middle of cookies plain to decorate for Santa's face.
Let frosting dry completely on wire racks. Decorate top of each cookie
with red icing to make a hat. Using white frosting to attach, add a
marshmallow quarter to hat for a pompom, 2 chocolate chip eyes and
a cinnamon candy nose. Let cookies dry completely on a wire rack
before serving. Makes about 2-1/2 dozen.

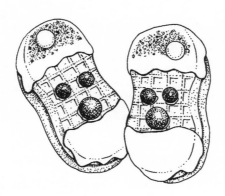

For a little pick-me-up gift, tuck a couple of Flo's Santa Cookies
and a packet of hot cocoa into a clear plastic tumbler. Wrap
in plastic wrap and tie with curling ribbon...sweet!

Quick Fruitcake Bites

Michelle Rooney
Gooseberry Patch

Use a mix of red & green cherries for a really festive look.

2 c. mini marshmallows
2 c. graham cracker crumbs
1 c. maraschino cherries,
  chopped

14-oz. can sweetened
  condensed milk
1/2 c. chopped pecans
3 c. sweetened flaked coconut

Combine all ingredients except coconut; mix well. Form dough into one-inch balls; roll in coconut. Chill for 3 hours, or until firm. Keep refrigerated in an airtight container. Makes about 5 dozen.

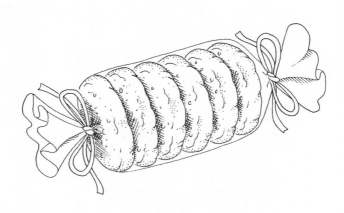

Fill a basket with "Christmas crackers" to set by the door...a take-home
treat for visitors! Roll a 4-inch length of paper towel tube in tissue
paper, extending 2 inches beyond ends. Fasten with a bit of tape.
Stack several bite-size cookies, wrap in plastic wrap and slip
inside each tube. Twist ends of tissue and tie with
narrow ribbon...clever!

Tropical Truffles

Rosa Lee Varady
Spring City, PA

Light, creamy and delicious.

8-oz. pkg. cream cheese,
   softened
8-oz. can crushed pineapple,
   drained

2-1/2 c. sweetened flaked
   coconut

Beat cream cheese and pineapple together. Cover and refrigerate for 30 minutes. Form into one-inch balls; roll in coconut. Refrigerate until ready to serve. Makes 2 dozen.

A whimsical gift for a beach-loving friend! Fill a mini beach pail
with Tropical Truffles. Wrap in clear plastic wrap and tuck a
paper parasol into the top...wind with a bright-colored
string of carnival beads in place of a ribbon.

Connie's Sandwich Cookies

Connie Hilty
Pearland, TX

Press on a chocolate drop with a bit of
frosting for a yummy finish.

16-1/2 oz. tube refrigerated
  peanut butter cookie dough
16-1/2 oz. tube refrigerated
  chocolate chip dough

1/2 c. creamy peanut butter
16-oz. container chocolate
  frosting

Slice each tube of dough into 36 equal pieces; roll into balls. Arrange balls 2 inches apart on ungreased baking sheets; flatten slightly in a criss-cross pattern with a fork dipped in sugar. Bake at 350 degrees for 8 to 11 minutes, until lightly golden. Cool on wire racks. Stir peanut butter into frosting until well blended; spread onto peanut butter cookies. Add chocolate chip cookies to form sandwiches; press gently. Chill until serving time. Makes 3 dozen.

To avoid overbaking, check cookies for doneness 2 to 3 minutes before the shorter baking time given. Cookies will continue to bake on the hot baking sheets even after removed from the oven.

1-2-3 Cookies

Ida Moore
Grants Pass, OR

*These couldn't be easier and they're delicious! They freeze
well for longer storage. I like chocolate cake mix...
my husband likes lemon cake mix.*

18-1/2 oz. pkg. favorite-flavor
    cake mix
1 egg, beaten

8-oz. container frozen whipped
    topping, thawed
1/2 c. powdered sugar

Mix together all ingredients except powdered sugar; form into one-
inch balls. Roll in powdered sugar; place on ungreased baking sheets.
Bake at 350 degrees for 12 to 15 minutes; cool. Makes about
6 dozen.

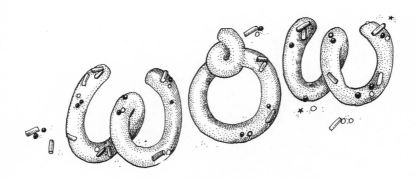

It's easy to decorate baked, unfrosted cookies with colored sugar
or sprinkles! Just use light corn syrup and a new paintbrush to
paint designs, then add sprinkles and shake off any excess.

Old-Time Skillet Cookies

Teri Austin
Jenks, OK

My mother used to make this recipe every year at Christmas...it always brings back good memories for me. My kids never knew her, but they have enjoyed many of the recipes she used to fix just for me.

1/2 c. butter
3/4 c. sugar
2 eggs, beaten
2 c. chopped dates
1 c. chopped pecans

1 t. vanilla extract
2 c. crispy rice cereal
3-1/2 oz. can sweetened flaked
   coconut

Combine butter, sugar and eggs in a large skillet over low heat; cook until butter is melted and sugar is well blended. Add chopped dates and cook for an additional 10 minutes. Remove from heat; stir in pecans and vanilla. Cool for 5 to 10 minutes; add cereal. Roll into walnut-size balls; roll in coconut. Store in airtight container. Makes 3-1/2 dozen.

For toasty flavor and color, simply spread shredded coconut on an ungreased baking sheet and bake for 5 to 7 minutes at 350 degrees.

Saucepan Cookies

Julie Hagen
Springfield, MO

*Serious comfort food! I come from a large family in Maine...
on cold winter days, these cookies were
so much fun to make and eat.*

1/2 c. butter
2 1-oz. sqs. unsweetened
   baking chocolate
1/2 c. milk
2 c. sugar

1/2 t. salt
1 t. vanilla extract
4 c. quick-cooking oats,
   uncooked

In a heavy saucepan over medium heat, melt butter and chocolate. Add milk, sugar and salt. Bring to a boil; boil for 2 minutes. Remove from heat. Add vanilla and oats; mix well. Drop by rounded tablespoonfuls onto wax paper to cool. Makes about 4 to 5 dozen.

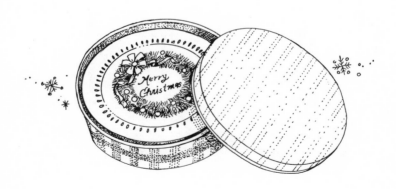

Decorate a cookie plate...perfect for entertaining or gift giving and oh-so easy! Stamp the back of a clear glass plate, using white or silver acrylic paint and a star-shaped foam craft stamp. Allow to dry, then set paint as indicated on label.

Butterscotch Crunchies

Tina Knotts
Gooseberry Patch

*Oh-so easy and unbelievably yummy! I like to stir in
some peanuts for extra crunch.*

2 c. butterscotch chips   3-1/2 c. corn flake cereal
1/4 c. creamy peanut butter

Melt butterscotch chips in a large saucepan over low heat. Add peanut
butter; stir in cereal. Drop by tablespoonfuls onto wax paper; cool.
Makes 2 dozen.

Whimsical ornaments that can double as gift tags! Trace around a favorite cookie cutter onto 2 layers of felt and cut out with pinking shears.
Stitch together simply or even use fabric glue, leaving an opening to
insert stuffing. Add the recipient's name in embroidery or fabric paint.

Graham No-Bake Cookies

Lisa Langston
Conroe, TX

A no-bake recipe that's a little different...I've never seen this version made with graham cracker crumbs anywhere else.

2 c. sugar
1/2 c. milk
2 T. baking cocoa
1/2 c. butter
1/2 c. creamy peanut butter

1 T. vanilla extract
2 c. quick-cooking oats, uncooked
1 c. graham cracker crumbs

Combine sugar, milk, cocoa and butter in a saucepan over medium heat. Bring to a boil for 2 minutes, stirring constantly. Remove from heat. Stir in peanut butter, vanilla, oats and crumbs; mix well. Drop by rounded tablespoonfuls onto buttered wax paper; cool completely. Makes 4 to 5 dozen.

Give a fresh new look to that old standby, no-bake cookies! Press cookie dough into a wax paper-lined baking pan and chill. When they're set, turn cookies out of pan, peel off wax paper and cut into diamond shapes.

Ladybug Cookies

Sherry Turpin
Carrollton, IL

My sons, Cody and Alex, and I created this recipe by adapting a
Gooseberry Patch *recipe for the basic instructions. When the cookies were baked, they looked like big ladybugs so we have named them Ladybug Cookies. They are very easy to make...everyone loves them!*

18-1/2 oz. pkg. red velvet
   cake mix
1/2 c. oil

2 eggs, beaten
12-oz. pkg. semi-sweet
   chocolate chips

Combine dry cake mix, oil and eggs; mix well. Stir in chocolate chips; drop by tablespoonfuls onto ungreased baking sheets. Bake at 350 degrees for 9 to 10 minutes. Makes 3-1/2 dozen.

Who took the cookie from the cookie jar?

-Old children's rhyme

TREATS IN A Twinkle

Peanut Butter Surprise Cookies

*Marta May
Anderson, IN*

Oh-so easy...just decorate with candy sprinkles for the holiday!

1 c. creamy peanut butter
1 sleeve round buttery crackers

2 12-oz. pkgs. semi-sweet or
  milk chocolate chips

Spread one tablespoon peanut butter on each cracker; set aside.
Place chocolate chips in a microwave-safe bowl. Microwave on high
setting for 2 to 3 minutes, stirring every 15 seconds, until melted.
With tongs, dip each cracker into melted chocolate, coating well.
Place on wax paper; let cool and harden. Store in an airtight container.
Makes 2 dozen.

Creamy Christmas Eggnog

*Regina Vining
Warwick, RI*

Garnish with freshly grated nutmeg...yum!

4 pasteurized eggs, separated
  and divided
5-oz. can evaporated milk
1 T. sugar

1 t. vanilla extract
4-1/2 c. milk
Optional: 2 T. rum

Beat egg yolks in a large bowl until thickened and light. Gradually stir
in evaporated milk, sugar, vanilla and milk. In a separate bowl, beat
egg whites until stiff peaks form; add to milk mixture. Stir in rum, if
desired. Makes 6 to 8 servings.

Cocoa Mocha Bites

Michelle Sheridan
Gooseberry Patch

Make 'em mini...roll into 1/2-inch balls for a
pop-in-your-mouth treat!

1/2 c. butter, softened
2/3 c. sugar
3 T. baking cocoa
1 T. strong brewed coffee

1/2 t. vanilla extract
1-3/4 c. quick-cooking oats,
   uncooked
1/3 c. powdered sugar

Blend together butter, sugar, cocoa, coffee and vanilla. Stir in oats;
mix well. Roll into one-inch balls. Dip balls into powdered sugar; place
on wax paper to set. Makes about 3 dozen.

Serve up cookie kabobs...fun for a dessert buffet. On wooden skewers,
alternate cookie balls with bite-size fresh or candied fruit pieces. Stand
skewers in a vase or insert them in a large styrofoam ball. Clever!

Cinnamon Cornmeal Cookies

Tonya Sheppard
Galveston, TX

Cinnamon baking chips are available in stores during the holiday season. Can't find them? Just use chocolate chips instead.

16-1/2 oz. tube refrigerated
   sugar cookie dough,
   softened
1/4 c. yellow cornmeal

20 mini chocolate candy bars
1/3 c. cinnamon baking chips
1 t. shortening

Break up cookie dough in a large bowl; knead in cornmeal until well blended. Wrap each candy bar in a rounded tablespoonful of dough, covering completely. Arrange 2 inches apart on lightly greased baking sheets. Bake at 375 degrees for 9 to 12 minutes, until edges are golden. Cool on baking sheets for one minute; remove to wire rack and cool completely. Combine cinnamon chips and shortening in a small microwave-safe bowl. Microwave on high for 30 to 45 seconds, stirring every 15 minutes, until smooth. Drizzle over cookies; let stand until set. Makes about 1-1/2 dozen.

Treat co-workers to deluxe sandwich cookies...ready in a twinkle!
Assemble extra-large cookies in pairs with creamy frosting
and roll edges in crushed candy canes...yummy!

Peanut Butter & Jam Bars

Angela Murphy
Tempe, AZ

Everyone's favorite flavors!

17-1/2 oz. pkg. peanut butter cookie mix	1/2 c. peanut butter chips
3 T. oil	16-oz. container vanilla frosting
1 T. water	1 T. milk
1 egg, beaten	1/4 c. creamy peanut butter
	1/4 c. strawberry jam

Combine cookie mix, oil, water and egg; stir into a soft dough. Add chips and mix well. Press dough into a lightly greased 13"x9" baking pan. Bake at 350 degrees for 15 to 18 minutes, until edges are light golden. Cool completely, about 30 minutes. Stir frosting, milk and peanut butter together until well blended. Spread over baked crust. Drop jam by teaspoonfuls over frosting mixture; swirl jam with a knife tip to create a marbled design. Refrigerate for 20 minutes, or until set. Slice into bars. Makes about 3 dozen.

Jams and preserves keep well, so pick up a few jars of local specialties like beach plum, peach or boysenberry on family vacations. Later, use them to bake up jam bars, linzer cookies or thumbprints... the flavors will bring back happy family memories!

Mmm...
CHOCOLATE

Ooey-Gooey Chocolate Tips

Check out what's new in the baking aisle...jazz up chocolate goodies in a jiffy! Try using swirled or flavored chocolate chips in your favorite chocolate chip cookie recipe. Or delight a chocolate lover by whipping up some fudge with premium-quality dark baking chocolate.

∘ ❊ ∘

Melt chocolate in the microwave...it's a snap! Place chocolate chips or baking squares in a microwave-safe container. Microwave on high setting for 30 to 60 seconds, stir, then microwave for another 15 seconds at a time just until chocolate softens.

∘ ❊ ∘

Flavoring extracts blend well with chocolate...how about raspberry, orange or peppermint?

∘ ❊ ∘

A drizzle of chocolate makes any homebaked cookie or candy extra special! Simply place chocolate chips in a small zipping bag and microwave briefly until melted. Snip off a tiny corner and squeeze to drizzle...afterwards, just toss away the bag.

Double Chocolate Brownies

Lauren Williams
Kewanee, MO

These made-from-scratch brownies are so good and easy...the icing makes each bite extra yummy. You will never use a box mix again!

1 c. chopped pecans
1-1/2 c. all-purpose flour, divided
2 c. sugar
10 T. baking cocoa, divided
1-1/2 c. margarine, melted and divided

4 eggs, beaten
1 t. vanilla extract
16-oz. pkg. powdered sugar
6 T. milk

Toss pecans with a little of the flour; set aside. Mix together remaining flour, sugar, 5 tablespoons cocoa, one cup margarine, eggs and vanilla. Stir in pecans; spread in a greased 11"x7" baking pan. Bake at 350 degrees for 30 minutes. For icing, combine powdered sugar, milk, remaining cocoa and remaining margarine; mix until smooth. Pour over brownies while hot. Cool; slice into squares. Makes 2 dozen.

Everybody loves tasty little brownie bites. Simply spoon batter into mini paper muffin liners and bake. Top each with a few milk chocolate chips while still warm...yum!

Buckeye Brownies

Karen McCann
Marion, OH

*Being from Ohio, with a son-in-law going to OSU, we are
naturally Buckeye fans. When the Ohio State Buckeyes
play, these brownies are a must!*

3/4 c. all-purpose flour
1/2 t. baking powder
1/2 t. salt
1/2 c. butter, softened and
  divided
6 T. baking cocoa

1 c. sugar
2 eggs, beaten
1-1/2 t. vanilla extract, divided
1/2 c. creamy peanut butter
1-1/4 c. powdered sugar
1 c. milk chocolate chips

Line an 8"x8" square baking pan with 2 crossed strips of aluminum
foil; spray with non-stick vegetable spray and set aside. Combine
flour, baking powder and salt; set aside. In a microwave-safe bowl,
melt 1/3 cup butter for one minute on high setting. Add cocoa, sugar,
eggs and one teaspoon vanilla; beat for one minute, until well
blended. Add dry ingredients; mix until combined. Spread in prepared
pan. Bake at 350 degrees for 20 minutes. Remove from oven;
let stand for 10 minutes. Mix peanut butter and remaining butter.
Add powdered sugar and remaining vanilla; mix until smooth.
Place mixture between 2 lengths of wax paper; roll out into an
8-inch by 8-inch square. Using foil strips as handles, remove
brownies from pan; set aside. Peel wax paper from top of peanut
butter mixture; turn onto top of brownies. Peel off remaining wax
paper. Melt chocolate chips and spread over top. Chill until firm,
about one hour. Cut into squares. Makes one dozen.

Decorate a paper sack in team colors
and fill with brownies. Fold the top
over, punch 2 holes and slide a mini
sports pennant through for a treat
any sports fan will love.

Italian Chocolate Cookies

Valeriejean Murphy
Windsor, CT

*My mother has made these cookies every
Christmas since I was a child.*

4 c. all-purpose flour
1/4 c. baking cocoa
2 t. ground cloves
2 t. cinnamon
2 t. nutmeg
2 T. baking powder
1/2 t. salt
1/2 c. shortening, melted

1-1/2 c. sugar
1 t. vanilla extract
1 c. warm brewed coffee
1 c. chopped nuts
1 c. raisins
1 c. powdered sugar
3 to 4 t. water

Combine flour, cocoa, spices, baking powder and salt; set aside. In a separate bowl, blend together shortening and sugar. Stir in vanilla extract and coffee; gradually add to flour mixture until well mixed. Stir in nuts and raisins. Form into one-inch balls and arrange on lightly greased baking sheets. Bake at 350 degrees for 10 minutes; cool. Mix together powdered sugar and water; drizzle over cookies. Makes 2 to 3 dozen.

Plump up raisins for extra moist, tender cookies! Soak them in warm water for 3 to 5 minutes, then drain before adding to recipe.

Layered Mint Chocolate Fudge

Andrea Schadel
Dighton, KS

I made this fudge for Thanksgiving at my in-laws' house. The fudge was a great hit...it was half gone before we got around to the turkey!

12-oz. pkg. semi-sweet chocolate chips
14-oz. can sweetened condensed milk, divided
2 t. vanilla extract

6-oz. pkg. white chocolate chips
1 T. peppermint extract
few drops green or red food coloring

Melt semi-sweet chocolate chips with one cup condensed milk in a heavy saucepan over low heat. Stir in vanilla. Spread half the mixture in a wax paper-lined 8"x8" baking pan; chill for 10 minutes, or until firm. Set aside remaining chocolate mixture at room temperature. In another heavy saucepan over low heat, melt white chocolate chips with remaining condensed milk. Stir in extract and desired food coloring. Spread over chilled chocolate layer; chill for 10 minutes, or until firm. Spread reserved chocolate mixture over mint layer. Chill for 2 hours, or until firm. Turn fudge onto cutting board; remove wax paper. Cut into squares. Store loosely covered at room temperature. Makes 1-3/4 pounds.

Fudge cut-outs are oh-so-simple to make and really dress up a dessert tray. Pour hot fudge into a jelly-roll pan and chill. Use mini cookie cutters to cut out stars, ornaments and other holiday shapes, then press on candy sprinkles or decorate with frosting. Yummy!

Chocolate Peppermint Drops

Diana Decker
Kerhonkson, NY

This is my own recipe. The cookies are so pretty and the flavor gets rave reviews from everyone who tastes them!

1 c. margarine, softened	2 c. all-purpose flour
2/3 c. sugar	3/4 c. baking cocoa
2/3 c. dark brown sugar, packed	1 t. baking soda
1 t. vanilla extract	1/2 t. salt
1 t. peppermint extract	1/2 c. candy canes, crushed
2 eggs, beaten	

Combine margarine, sugars, extracts and eggs in a large bowl; mix well. Add remaining ingredients except candy canes; blend well. Chill for 15 minutes, or until dough is easy to handle. Roll well-rounded teaspoons of dough into balls; place on parchment paper-lined baking sheets. Bake at 325 degrees for 11 to 13 minutes, or until cookies are puffed and centers are set. Remove from oven; with the back of a spoon, immediately and gently make a well in center of cookies. Spoon about 1/2 teaspoon of crushed candy into well. Let stand for 2 to 3 minutes before removing from baking sheet. Makes 3-1/2 dozen.

Treat a book lover to a gift basket packed just for her! Fill it with her favorite books, a bookmark, a clip-on reading light, a fun coffee mug, gourmet coffee or tea and of course a package of homebaked cookies. She'll love you for it!

Minty Chocolate Cookies

Diana Krol
Nickerson, KS

So quick & easy...especially festive on a holiday cookie platter!

18-1/2 oz. pkg. devil's food
   cake mix
2 eggs, beaten

1/2 c. oil
1 c. candy canes, crushed

Mix together dry cake mix, eggs and oil; gently stir in crushed candy. Drop by tablespoonfuls onto lightly greased baking sheets. Bake at 350 degrees for about 10 minutes; do not overbake. Makes 3-1/2 dozen.

Caramel Chocolate Pretzels

A sweet & salty treat to pack in vintage canning jars! Simply dip pretzel rods in melted chocolate. Drizzle with a different color chocolate, then roll in chopped nuts, crushed candy canes or candy sprinkles for a dazzling candy-shop pretzel that's so easy to do. (Shh...we won't tell!)

Chocolate-Pecan Biscotti

Stella Hickman
Gooseberry Patch

Crunchy and oh-so-dunkable!

1/2 c. butter, softened
2/3 c. powdered low-calorie
   sugar blend for baking
1/4 c. baking cocoa
2 t. baking powder

3 eggs, beaten
1-3/4 c. all-purpose flour
1/4 c. chopped pecans
1/2 c. sugar-free chocolate
   candy, chopped

Beat butter in a large bowl for 30 seconds. Add sugar blend, cocoa and baking powder; beat until well combined. Blend in eggs until well mixed. Beat in as much flour as possible; stir in remaining flour by hand with wooden spoon. Stir in nuts and candy. Divide dough in half; roll into two, 9-inch long rolls. Arrange on greased baking sheets; flatten rolls to 2 inches wide. Bake at 375 degrees for 20 to 25 minutes; cool on baking sheets for one hour. Place rolls on a cutting board; slice 1/2-inch thick. Return slices cut-side down to baking sheets; bake at 325 degrees for 8 minutes. Flip over and bake for an additional 7 to 9 minutes. Cool on rack. Makes about 2-1/2 dozen.

Wrap several biscotti in festive cellophane and tie with curling ribbons to a package of gourmet coffee beans...a coffee lover's delight!

Chocolate-Peanut Butter Balls

Marilyn Miller
Fort Washington, PA

Roll in crushed peanuts for extra nuttiness.

1/2 c. butter
18-oz. jar creamy peanut butter
16-oz. pkg. powdered sugar

3-1/2 c. crispy rice cereal
18-oz. pkg. milk chocolate bar,
   chopped

Melt butter in a large saucepan over medium heat. Blend in peanut butter; stir in powdered sugar and cereal. Form into one-inch balls and place on wax paper. Melt chocolate on top of double boiler. Dip balls in chocolate to coat; arrange on baking sheets to cool and set. Makes about 5 dozen.

Put that melon baller to year 'round use! It's just the tool for
for scooping chocolate candy into balls for truffles.

Chocolate-Orange Snowballs

Beth Kramer
Port Saint Lucie, FL

Florida orange juice and Georgia pecans make these my favorite
way to share a little sunshine with friends up north.

9-oz. pkg. vanilla wafers
2-1/4 c. powdered sugar,
   divided
1/4 c. baking cocoa

1/4 c. light corn syrup
1/3 c. frozen orange juice
   concentrate, thawed
1-1/2 c. chopped pecans

In a food processor, combine vanilla wafers, 2 cups powdered sugar,
cocoa, corn syrup and orange juice concentrate. Process until wafers
are finely ground and mixture is well blended. Add pecans and
process until nuts are finely chopped. Transfer mixture to a bowl;
form into one-inch balls. Roll in remaining powdered sugar. Store
in an airtight container. Makes about 5 dozen.

Allow chocolate truffles to stand at room temperature
for 15 minutes before serving for extra creaminess.

Chocolotta Pizza

Rebecca Mosher
Crossett, AR

*I got this recipe from a good friend of mine and made a
few additions so it's even richer. Everyone just loves it!*

12-oz. pkg. semi-sweet
  chocolate chips
8 2-oz. squares white melting
  chocolate, divided
2 c. mini marshmallows
1 c. crispy rice cereal

6-oz. jar maraschino cherries,
  drained and halved
16-oz. pkg. candy-coated
  chocolate peanuts
1 t. oil

Combine chocolate chips and 7 squares white chocolate in a 2-quart
microwave-safe bowl. Microwave on high setting for 2 minutes; stir.
Microwave an additional one to 2 minutes, until smooth, stirring
every 30 seconds. Stir in marshmallows and cereal. Spoon onto a
greased 12" pizza pan. Top with cherries and peanuts, pressing gently.
Microwave remaining white chocolate with oil for one minute; stir.
Microwave for 30 seconds to one minute, until smooth, stirring every
15 seconds. Drizzle over pizza; chill until firm. Refrigerate until ready
to serve. Let stand at room temperature for 10 to 15 minutes before
slicing into wedges. Makes 10 to 12 servings.

Present a Chocolotta Pizza in a new pizza box...tie on
a new pizza cutter for slicing.

Brownie Pizza Slices

Sandra Paananen
Howell, MI

I have made this recipe for socials and it always disappears in minutes! Everyone likes a different topping on their brownie, so garnishing the wedges individually makes everybody happy.

1 c. butter, divided
1-1/2 c. sugar
1-1/2 t. vanilla extract
3 eggs, beaten
3/4 c. baking cocoa, divided
3/4 c. all-purpose flour
1/2 t. baking powder

1/4 t. salt
1-1/2 c. powdered sugar
2 to 3 T. milk
Garnish: mini chocolate chips,
   peanut butter candies,
   toasted coconut, toffee
   baking bits, chopped pecans

Melt 3/4 cup butter; beat together with sugar, vanilla and eggs. Stir in 1/2 cup cocoa, flour, baking powder and salt just until moistened. Spread into a greased 9" pie plate. Bake at 350 degrees for 16 to 20 minutes; do not overbake. Test for doneness after 16 minutes. Remove from oven; cool for 10 minutes. Combine remaining butter, powdered sugar, milk and remaining cocoa. Spread over brownie in a thin, smooth layer. With a sharp knife, cut brownie into 8 wedges. Carefully remove each wedge and place on a wire rack. Sprinkle wedges with a variety of garnishes, or leave plain. Wrap each wedge in plastic wrap or wax paper. Makes 8 servings.

For a chocolatey topping in an instant, sprinkle brownies with chocolate chips as soon as they come out of the oven. When chips soften, spread them with a spatula. Yum!

Caramel Pecan Turtles

Tracey Varela
Thomasville, GA

*There's nothing slow about the way these turtles
disappear from a candy tray!*

1 c. pecan halves
36 vanilla caramels

1/2 c. semi-sweet chocolate
chips

On an oiled baking sheet, arrange 5 pecans together to create turtle legs and head. Place one caramel in the center of each turtle. Repeat with remaining pecans and caramels. Bake at 325 degrees for 5 to 10 minutes, until caramels are soft. Remove from oven and flatten caramel centers with a spatula. Melt chocolate chips in a saucepan over low heat; spoon over caramel centers. Cool until set. Makes about 2-1/2 dozen.

Create a gingerbread house the easy way...no baking, just fun! Choose a small house-shaped box from the neighborhood craft store or an empty food container, then turn everyone's imagination loose with decorator frostings, assorted candies, even cereal and pretzels! Kids love this...just be sure to have extra candies on hand for nibbling.

Creamy Chocolate Pecans

Kim Conner
South Boston, VA

*I make a lot of candy for Christmas, so I keep my chocolate
melting pot handy...it works something like a
slow cooker to melt chocolate easily.*

4 egg yolks
2/3 c. whipping cream
2/3 c. sugar
1-2/3 c. semi-sweet chocolate
   chips

1 t. vanilla extract
1/2 lb. pecan halves
14-oz. pkg. milk chocolate for
   melting

Beat egg yolks until thick and lemon colored; add cream and sugar.
Cook in top of a double boiler over low heat until very thick. Place
semi-sweet chocolate in a microwave-safe bowl. Microwave on high
for about 1-1/2 minutes, stirring every 15 seconds; cool slightly and
add to egg mixture. Stir in vanilla; beat well and chill. Form into small
balls; press a pecan half onto each side (2 pecans per ball). Place milk
chocolate in a microwave-safe bowl. Microwave on high setting for
one to 2 minutes, stirring every 15 seconds until melted. Dip balls into
melted chocolate; cool on wax paper. Makes about 3 dozen.

Pick up some extra disposable icing cones when you shop for baking
supplies. Filled with small treats, tied with ribbon and placed in
a wire cupcake stand, they make sweet gifts to keep
on hand for Christmas visitors.

Chocolate Caramels

Diana Chaney
Olathe, KS

Is there anything more tempting than old-fashioned homemade caramels? Yes...caramels with chocolate added!

1-1/2 c. whipping cream
1 c. sugar
3/4 c. light corn syrup

3 1-oz. sqs. semi-sweet baking
   chocolate, chopped
1/4 t. salt

Combine all ingredients in a heavy saucepan over low heat. Cook, stirring constantly, until mixture thickens and reaches the firm-ball stage, or 244 to 249 degrees on a candy thermometer. Pour into a lightly buttered 8"x4" loaf pan without scraping bottom of saucepan. Let stand until set. Score candy into 48 squares with a knife. Turn candy out onto a cool surface; turn over so scored side is up. Cut into squares along scored lines. Wrap each caramel in a square of wax paper. Let stand in a cool place overnight; store at room temperature. Makes about 4 dozen.

A recipe for success...always make candy just one batch at a time. Don't be tempted to double or triple the recipe, because the candy may fail to set up properly. (Although eating syrupy fudge directly from the spoon can be a guilty pleasure in itself!)

Espresso Bean Bark

Stacie Mickley
Gooseberry Patch

Try using your favorite flavored coffee beans...irresistible!

12-oz. pkg. semi-sweet
  chocolate chips
1 t. margarine

3/4 c. whole coffee beans
1/4 c. white melting chocolate,
  chopped

Combine chocolate chips and margarine in a microwave-safe bowl. Microwave on high setting for 2 to 3 minutes, stirring every 30 seconds, until melted and smooth. Stir in coffee beans until evenly distributed. Pour onto a wax paper-lined baking sheet; spread evenly. Sprinkle with white chocolate; press lightly. Freeze until set, about 5 minutes. Break into pieces; store in an airtight container. Makes about 12 servings.

Use short lengths of red licorice strings to hang sugar cookie ornaments from tree branches...clever!

Tex-Mex Chocolate Snappers

Cathy Clemons
Narrows, VA

*I attended a class reunion in Texas and came back with
this terrific recipe. We brought goodies to share
at the hotel and this was a favorite...yum!*

1-3/4 c. all-purpose flour	3/4 c. butter, softened
2 t. baking soda	1 egg, beaten
1 t. cinnamon	1/4 c. light corn syrup
1/4 t. salt	2 1-oz. envs. pre-melted
1-1/2 c. sugar, divided	unsweetened chocolate

Combine flour, baking soda, cinnamon and salt. In a separate bowl,
beat together one cup sugar, butter and egg until creamy. Add corn
syrup and pre-melted chocolate. Stir in flour mixture and shape into
one-inch balls. Roll balls in remaining sugar to coat; place on ungreased baking sheets. Bake for 12 to 15 minutes. Makes 2 dozen.

Fill vintage Mason jars with old-fashioned hard candies and line them
up across your mantel...an instant glad-you-came gift for guests.

Coconut Bon-Bons

Carol Lytle
Columbus, OH

You'll have a little extra condensed milk left over...
stir it into hot coffee for a wonderful treat!

1/4 c. butter, softened
16-oz. pkg. powdered sugar
1 c. sweetened condensed milk
2 c. sweetened flaked coconut

9 1-oz. sqs. semi-sweet
   chocolate
2 T. shortening

Mix together butter, powdered sugar and condensed milk. Stir in coconut. Roll into one-inch balls; refrigerate until set, about one hour. Melt chocolate and shortening in a double boiler over medium heat, stirring occasionally until smooth. Remove from heat; stir until well blended. With a toothpick, dip balls into chocolate to coat. Set on wax paper to dry. Makes about 3 dozen.

Make a truffle tree...yum! Cover a cone-shaped foam tree form with truffles, using toothpicks to fasten them on.

Cookies & Vanilla Cream Fudge

Megan Brooks
Antioch, TN

Creamy, crunchy chocolate...divine!

3 6-oz. pkgs. white chocolate
   chips
14-oz. can sweetened
   condensed milk

1/8 t. salt
2 c. chocolate sandwich cookies,
   coarsely crushed

Melt chocolate, condensed milk and salt in a heavy saucepan over low heat; stir until smooth. Remove from heat; stir in cookies. Spread evenly in a greased aluminum foil-lined 8"x8" baking pan. Chill for 2 hours, or until firm. Turn fudge onto cutting board; peel off foil and cut into squares. Store tightly covered at room temperature. Makes about 3-1/2 dozen.

Pile squares of scrumptious fudge under a clear glass dome...
oh-so inviting for guests to sample!

Mmm...**CHOCOLATE**

Mocha Pecan Fudge

Samantha Starks
Madison, WI

*For bite-size bon-bons, scoop warm fudge with a
mini melon baller. Roll balls in a mixture of
powdered sugar and baking cocoa. Mmm!*

1 c. chopped pecans
3 6-oz. pkgs. semi-sweet
   chocolate chips
14-oz. can sweetened
   condensed milk

2 T. strong brewed coffee,
   cooled
1 t. cinnamon
1/8 t. salt
1 t. vanilla extract

Place pecans in a microwave-safe pie plate. Microwave, uncovered,
on high for 4 minutes, stirring after each minute; set aside. In a large
microwave-safe bowl, combine chocolate chips, condensed milk,
coffee, cinnamon and salt. Microwave, uncovered, on high for
1-1/2 minutes. Stir until smooth. Stir in vanilla and pecans;
immediately spread in a greased aluminum foil-lined 8"x8" baking
pan. Cover and refrigerate until firm, about 2 hours. Remove from
pan; cut into one-inch squares. Cover and store at room temperature.
Makes about 5 dozen.

A sweet way to give a gift of fudge! Press a cookie cutter into freshly
made fudge to fill it completely, lift out (cookie cutter and all) and chill.
Wrap in festive cellophane and tie with a sparkly ribbon...sweet!

Morgan's Crinkle Cookies

Morgan Kame
Mounds, OK

An old-fashioned favorite.

1/2 c. oil
1/4 c. butter
10 T. baking cocoa
2 c. sugar
2 eggs

1 t. vanilla extract
2 c. all-purpose flour
2 t. baking powder
1 t. salt
1 c. powdered sugar

Combine oil, butter, cocoa and sugar in a large bowl. Beat in eggs, one at a time, until well blended; add vanilla. Stir in flour, baking powder and salt. Chill for 2 hours. Form into one-inch balls and roll in powdered sugar. Arrange on greased baking sheets. Bake at 350 degrees for 8 to 10 minutes. Makes 6-1/2 dozen.

Give fresh-baked cookies whenever you like! Make and freeze extra cookie dough to share later...just remember to tuck in a card with the recipe name and baking instructions.

Trillionaire Cookies

Becky Kuchenbecker
Ravenna, OH

Make a dollar-bill bow! Pinch 3 crisp play-money bills in the center and twist with a pipe cleaner, then fluff out bills and tape to a package of Trillionaire Cookies...fun!

12-oz. jar caramel ice cream
   topping
1 c. pecans, finely chopped

36 round buttery crackers
12-oz. pkg. semi-sweet
   chocolate chips

Combine caramel topping and pecans in a saucepan over medium heat, stirring constantly. Bring to a boil and cook for 3 to 5 minutes, until mixture thickens; remove from heat. Arrange crackers on a wax paper-lined baking sheet. Spoon about 1-1/2 teaspoons caramel mixture onto each cracker. Refrigerate for one hour, or until firm. In a small saucepan, melt chocolate over low heat, stirring constantly. Remove from heat. With tongs, dip each cracker in melted chocolate up to the caramel filling; do not dip filling. Return to baking sheet. With a slotted spoon, drizzle melted chocolate over cookies. Refrigerate for one hour, or until chocolate is firm. Keep refrigerated in an airtight container. Makes 3 dozen.

Stir a tablespoon each of chocolate syrup and caramel topping into a cup of hot coffee. Top with a dollop of whipped topping.

Chocolate Truffle Cookies

Angie Biggin
Lyons, IL

Oh-so rich...a real chocolate lover's cookie!

1-1/4 c. butter, softened
2-1/4 c. powdered sugar
1/3 c. baking cocoa
1/4 c. sour cream

1 t. vanilla extract
2-1/4 c. all-purpose flour
12-oz. pkg. semi-sweet
    chocolate chips

Blend together butter, powdered sugar and cocoa. Mix in sour cream and vanilla; add flour and mix well. Stir in chocolate chips. Chill for one hour. Form dough into one-inch balls; arrange 2 inches apart on ungreased baking sheets. Bake at 325 degrees for 15 minutes, or until set. Cool for at least 10 minutes on wire racks. Makes 2 dozen.

Give your favorite chocolate recipe a delectable cherry flavor...
simply replace some of the vanilla extract with almond extract.

Chocolate Bit Meringues

Laina Lamb
Bucyrus, OH

I created these for my daughter Chelsea's 10th birthday party to have light treats to send home with her guests. They are so yummy...a crispy shell with creamy chocolate chips inside. We like to make them anytime it's not humid.

4 egg whites, at room
    temperature
1/2 t. cream of tartar
1 t. vanilla extract

3 T. baking cocoa
1 c. sugar
1 c. mini semi-sweet chocolate
    chips

With an electric mixer on high speed, beat egg whites in a large bowl until stiff. Add cream of tartar and beat until stiff peaks form. Add vanilla, cocoa and sugar. Fold in mini chocolate chips. Drop by tablespoonfuls onto aluminum foil-lined baking sheets. Bake at 250 degrees for one hour and 15 minutes, or until set and dry. Allow to cool on baking sheets. Store in an airtight container. Makes 3 dozen.

Decorate a frosty glass jar to fill with holiday goodies. Choose a clear glass jar and press on star or snowflake-shaped stickers as desired. Following package directions, apply etching cream to jar, covering completely. Peel off stickers when finished to reveal your one-of-a-kind design!!

Peanut Butter-Chocolate Fingers

Peggy Helm
Louisville, KY

I remember Grandma Kempf would always cut these into
great big 4-inch squares...we loved them!

1/2 c. margarine, softened
1/2 c. sugar
1/2 c. brown sugar, packed
1 egg, beaten
1/3 c. creamy peanut butter
1 c. quick-cooking oats,
  uncooked

1 c. all-purpose flour
1/2 t. baking soda
1/4 t. salt
1/2 t. vanilla extract
6-oz. pkg. semi-sweet chocolate
  chips

Combine margarine, sugars, egg and peanut butter; mix well. Add oats, flour, baking soda and salt; stir in vanilla. Pour into a lightly greased 13"x9" baking pan. Bake at 350 degrees for 20 to 25 minutes. Immediately sprinkle with chocolate chips. Let stand until chocolate is melted; spread evenly. Chill for 10 to 15 minutes, until chocolate is set. Spread with frosting. Cut into rectangular "fingers." Makes 3 dozen small bars or 2 dozen larger bars.

Frosting:

1/2 c. powdered sugar
1/4 c. peanut butter

2 to 4 t. milk

Combine all ingredients; mix until smooth.

Double Fudgy Cookie Bars

Vickie

*Be sure to have a big pitcher of icy cold milk
to serve with these rich, crunchy treats.*

24 chocolate sandwich cookies,
    divided
1/4 c. butter, melted
12-oz. pkg. semi-sweet
    chocolate chips, divided

14-oz. can sweetened
    condensed milk
1 t. vanilla extract

Place 18 cookies in a food processor; process to coarse crumbs. Set aside remaining cookies. Combine cookie crumbs and melted butter in a small bowl until well blended. Press into an ungreased 13"x11" baking pan; set aside. Combine one cup chocolate chips, condensed milk and vanilla. Melt in a double boiler over medium heat, stirring frequently until smooth. Spread chocolate mixture carefully over crumb crust; sprinkle with remaining chocolate chips. Break remaining cookies into pieces by hand; sprinkle over top. Bake at 325 degrees for 20 to 25 minutes. Refrigerate until chilled completely; cut into bars. Makes 20.

Blessed with lots of co-workers to share the holiday spirit with?
Surprise each of them with a single yummy, super-size
cookie bar, drizzled with chocolate and candy sprinkles.
Wrap in shiny cellophane...cheers!

North Pole Candy Cane Fudge

Sharon Tillman
Hampton, VA

Sprinkle extra crushed candy over the top for a pretty finish.

2 10-oz. pkgs. white chocolate
   chips
14-oz. can sweetened
   condensed milk

1/2 t. peppermint extract
1-1/2 c. candy canes, crushed
1/8 t. red food coloring

Combine chocolate chips and condensed milk in a saucepan over low heat. Stir until nearly melted; remove from heat and continue to stir until smooth and completely melted. Sir in extract, crushed candy and coloring. Spread evenly in an aluminum foil-lined, greased 8"x8" baking pan. Chill for 2 hours; cut into one-inch squares. Makes 64 pieces.

For a sweet greeting, pour North Pole Candy Cane Fudge into small, shallow disposable baking pans. After fudge sets, pipe on a holiday greeting with colored icing. Wrap in clear cellophane and hand-deliver as edible Christmas cards...yum!

Cool Mint Chocolate Swirls

Lynn Williams
Muncie, IN

Chocolatey cookies topped with a cool, refreshing mint wafer.

3/4 c. butter
1-1/2 c. brown sugar, packed
2 T. water
12-oz. pkg. semi-sweet
   chocolate chips
2 eggs

2-1/2 c. all-purpose flour
1-1/4 t. baking soda
1/2 t. salt
3 4-1/2 oz. pkgs. crème de
   menthe wafer thins

In a saucepan over medium heat, combine butter, brown sugar and water. Cook, stirring occasionally, until melted. Remove from heat. Stir in chocolate chips until melted; cool for 10 minutes. Pour chocolate mixture into a large bowl; beat in eggs, one at a time. In a separate bowl, combine flour, baking soda and salt; stir into chocolate mixture. Chill dough for at least one hour. Form into walnut-size balls; place 2 inches apart on greased baking sheets. Bake at 350 degrees for 8 to 10 minutes; do not overbake. Press a mint wafer onto each cookie while still warm; let stand for one minute. When mint softens, swirl mint over cookie with a spoon. Makes 3 to 4 dozen.

Make holiday cookies and candies look magical. Sprinkle on edible glitter, confetti and colorful sugar...oh-so sparkly!

213

Cocoa Buttercream Frosting

Tina Wright
Atlanta, GA

Perfect for sugar cookies!

1/4 c. butter
2 c. powdered sugar
3 T. baking cocoa

1 t. vanilla extract
2 to 3 T. milk

Mix together all ingredients except milk. Add milk, a little at a time, until a smooth frosting consistency is reached. Makes about one cup.

Homemade Hot Cocoa

Judy Dobiecki
Avondale, AZ

Treat yourself! Garnish with a dollop of whipped topping and a peppermint stick stirrer.

1 c. milk
2 T. baking cocoa

1/8 t. salt
2 T. sugar

Combine ingredients in a small saucepan over medium-low heat. Cook and stir until hot and bubbly. Pour into a mug. Serves one.

The world is so full of a number of things,
I'm sure we should all be as happy as kings.

-Robert Louis Stevenson

Nutty Butterscotch Crunch

Lynda Robson
Boston, MA

Part cookie, part candy]...yum!

12-oz. pkg. semi-sweet
   chocolate chips
11-1/2 oz. pkg. butterscotch
   chips

2-1/2 c. dry-roasted peanuts
4 c. chow mein noodles

Melt together chocolate and butterscotch chips in the top of a double boiler over simmering water. Remove from heat; add peanuts. Stir in noodles until well coated. Press into a buttered 13"x9" baking pan. Chill until set; cut into squares. Makes 2 dozen.

Nutty Butterscotch Crunch can also be made into charming "bird nests." Instead of pressing the mixture into a pan, drop by generous tablespoonfuls onto wax paper. Press 2 or 3 jelly beans onto each cluster.

Rocky Road Fudge

Holly Curry
Grahamsville, NY

*My husband's all-time favorite candy. If it were up to him,
this recipe would say, "Makes just one serving!"*

12-oz. pkg. semi-sweet
   chocolate chips
14-oz. can sweetened
   condensed milk

2 T. butter
3 c. dry-roasted peanuts
10-1/2 oz. pkg. mini
   marshmallows

Mix chocolate chips, condensed milk and butter in a saucepan over
medium heat. Cook and stir until melted. Remove from heat; add
peanuts and marshmallows. Spread in a greased 13"x9" baking pan.
Chill until firm; cut into squares. Makes 3-1/4 pounds.

A little coffee brings out the flavor in any chocolate recipe. Just dissolve
a tablespoon of instant coffee granules in liquid ingredients
and continue as directed.

Choco-Nut Dainties

Gloria Kaufmann
Orrville, OH

*I like to take this cookie to cookie swaps at Christmas...everyone
loves chocolate chip cookies! Shaped into logs, with the ends
dipped in chocolate and nuts, they look so special.*

1 c. margarine, softened and
    divided
3/4 c. sugar
1 egg, beaten
1-1/2 t. vanilla extract
2-1/4 c. all-purpose flour

1/2 t. salt
6-oz. pkg. semi-sweet chocolate
    chips
12-oz. pkg. semi-sweet
    chocolate chips
Optional: 1 c. chopped walnuts

Beat together 3/4 cup margarine, sugar, egg and vanilla in a large
bowl until well mixed. Add flour and salt; stir in smaller package of
chocolate chips. On a lightly floured surface, shape dough into 2-inch
by 1/2-inch logs. Arrange on ungreased baking sheets. Bake at
350 degrees for 12 to 15 minutes; cool on wire racks. Combine
remaining margarine and larger package of chocolate chips in a
double boiler over medium heat. Stir until melted and smooth; remove
from heat. Dip ends of cookies into melted chocolate; roll in chopped
nuts, if desired. Place on wax paper until set. Makes about
1-1/2 dozen.

Don't forget the camera on family cookie baking day! Snapshots
of children's little hands cutting out cookies, sweet faces smudged
with frosting and gorgeous platters of decorated cookies
will be cherished for years to come.

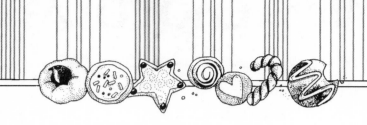

For twice the fun, create new cookie shapes using cookie cutters already in your cupboard! These ideas will get you started...can you think of others?

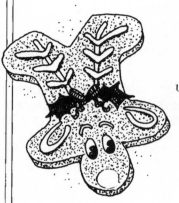

Reindeer cookies...

Flip a gingerbread man cookie upside-down. Pipe on antlers, ears and a face, and add a bright red gumdrop nose.

Santa cookies...

Turn star-shaped cookies into jolly Santas! Spread with red frosting, leaving faces unfrosted. Add flaked coconut for the beard, then dip the star's tips in chocolate frosting for mittens and boots.

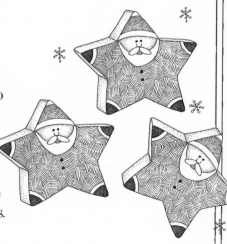

Simple Snowman cookies...

A plain round cookie becomes a
happy snowman! Cover him in
fluffy white frosting and add candy
sprinkle features...use a strip of
fruit roll-ups for his muffler.

Mini Gift Box cookies...

Simple square cookies become
tiny gifts when you
pipe on frosting ribbons.
Keep 'em simple or add dots
or stripes in fun colors.

Merry Reindeer cookies...

Turn a bell-shaped cookie
upside-down and press on
mini pretzel twists for antlers...
add chocolate chip eyes
and a candy nose.

INDEX

INDEX

INDEX

We've cooked up a whole collection of **Gooseberry Patch** ® books!

Have a taste for more? Call us toll-free at
1-800-854-6673
We'll send you our latest catalog filled with kitchenware, handmade quilts, gourmet goodies, enamelware, mixing bowls, night lights and our very own line of cookbooks, calendars and organizers!

Phone us:
1·800·854·6673

Fax us:
1·740·363·7225

Visit our website:
www.gooseberrypatch.com

Send us your favorite recipe!

and the memory that makes it special for you![*] If we select your recipe for a brand-new **Gooseberry Patch** cookbook, your name will appear right along with it...and you'll receive a FREE copy of the book! Submit your recipe on our website at **www.gooseberrypatch.com** or mail to:

Gooseberry Patch
Attn: Cookbook Dept.
P.O. Box 190
Delaware, OH 43015

*Please include the number of servings and all other necessary information!

spicy gingerbread men ✻ fluffy frosting

Mom's sugar cookies cookie swaps

cinnamon & ginger · cookies for Santa

sugary sprinkles · sparkly gumdrops

U.S. to Canadian recipe equivalents

Volume Measurements

1/4 teaspoon	1 mL
1/2 teaspoon	2 mL
1 teaspoon	5 mL
1 tablespoon = 3 teaspoons	15 mL
2 tablespoons = 1 fluid ounce	30 mL
1/4 cup	60 mL
1/3 cup	75 mL
1/2 cup = 4 fluid ounces	125 mL
1 cup = 8 fluid ounces	250 mL
2 cups = 1 pint =16 fluid ounces	500 mL
4 cups = 1 quart	1 L

Weights

1 ounce	30 g
4 ounces	120 g
8 ounces	225 g
16 ounces = 1 pound	450 g

Oven Temperatures

300° F	150° C
325° F	160° C
350° F	180° C
375° F	190° C
400° F	200° C
450° F	230° C

Baking Pan Sizes

Square

8x8x2 inches	2 L = 20x20x5 cm
9x9x2 inches	2.5 L = 23x23x5 cm

Rectangular

13x9x2 inches	3.5 L = 33x23x5 cm

Loaf

9x5x3 inches	2 L = 23x13x7 cm

Round

8x1-1/2 inches	1.2 L = 20x4 cm
9x1-1/2 inches	1.5 L = 23x4 cm